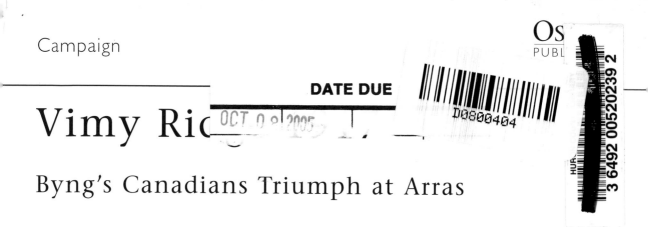

Campaign

# Vimy Ridge

## Byng's Canadians Triumph at Arras

DATE DUE

OCT 0 9 2005

D0800404

Os PUBL

HUR

3 6492 00520239 2

940.431 Tur

Turner, A.
Vimy Ridge 1917.

PRICE: $27.95 (3559/go   )

Campaign · 151

OSPREY
PUBLISHING

# Vimy Ridge 1917

## Byng's Canadians Triumph at Arras

Alexander Turner · Illustrated by Peter Dennis

Series editor Lee Johnson

First published in Great Britain in 2005 by Osprey Publishing, Midland House, West Way, Botley, Oxford OX2 0PH, United Kingdom.
Email: info@ospreypublishing.com

© 2005 Osprey Publishing Ltd.

All rights reserved. Apart from any fair dealing for the purpose of private study, research, criticism or review, as permitted under the Copyright, Designs and Patents Act, 1988, no part of this publication may be reproduced, stored in a retrieval system, or transmitted in any form or by any means, electronic, electrical, chemical, mechanical, optical, photocopying, recording or otherwise, without the prior written permission of the copyright owner. Enquiries should be addressed to the Publishers.

ISBN 1 84176 871 5

Editor: Ilios Publishing, Oxford, UK (www.iliospublishing.com)
Design: The Black Spot
Index by Alison Worthington
Maps by The Map Studio Ltd.
3D bird's eye views by The Black Spot
Battlescene artwork by Peter Dennis
Originated by PPS-Grasmere Ltd, Leeds, UK
Printed in China through World Print Ltd.

05 06 07 08 09   10 9 8 7 6 5 4 3 2 1

A CIP catalogue record for this book is available from the British Library.

For a catalogue of all books published by Osprey Military and Aviation please contact:

NORTH AMERICA
Osprey Direct, 2427 Bond Street, University Park, IL 60466, USA
E-mail: info@ospreydirectusa.com

ALL OTHER REGIONS
Osprey Direct UK, P.O. Box 140, Wellingborough,
Northants, NN8 2FA, UK
E-mail: info@ospreydirect.co.uk

**www.ospreypublishing.com**

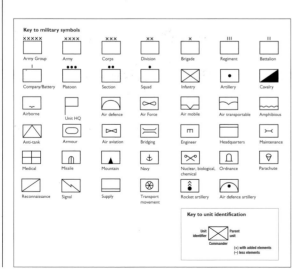

# Dedication

To Alan, for always setting the right example.

# Acknowledgements

I thank the Commanding Officer of 1st Battalion Irish Guards, Lt. Col. Charlie Knaggs, for giving me all the time required to research and write this book. I am also grateful for the considerable assistance and advice from Lt. Col. (Retired) Phillip Robinson of the Durrand Group, Dr Ernst Aichner of the Bayerisches Armeemuseum, Oberleutnant Kesselring from the Militärgeschichtliches Forschungsamt in Potsdam and all the staff at the Imperial War Museum, National Army Museum and National Archives. I am indebted to my friends Tom Earl (for flying me in tedious circles around Vimy Ridge) and Crispin Daly (for his German language ability). Simon Millar and Lee Johnson must receive the last word for all their wisdom and enthusiasm.

# Author's note

In describing military formations, the text of this narrative conforms to the convention of only using capital letters in the title of units. Generic references to armies, corps, divisions, brigades, battalions and companies remain in the lower case as demonstrated here. Where denoting a numbered battalion within a regiment, it will read (for example) 1st/263rd. Unless otherwise specified, all photographs are reproduced with the permission of the Imperial War Museum.

# Artist's note

Readers may care to note that the original paintings from which the colour plates in this book were prepared are available for private sale. The Publishers retain all reproduction copyright whatsoever. All enquiries should be addressed to:

Peter Dennis, The Park, Mansfield, Notts, NG18 2AT

The Publishers regret that they can enter into no correspondence upon this matter.

# CONTENTS

# INTRODUCTION

LEFT **Mother Canada. The olive branch in her right hand represents the 1919 Armistice. (Author's collection)**

BELOW **A French *poilu* on Vimy Ridge in December 1915. Despite incredible bravery, the repeated attempts of the French to capture the ridge proved futile. Indeed, the position in this photograph was taken by the Germans the following January. The trench appears dry because it is frozen. (IWM Q49225)**

Her head tilted in mute reflection, a grief-stricken Mother Canada stands alone on Vimy Ridge, mourning the loss of her adored sons. Nowhere on the Western Front is there a more potent memorial to the generation of young men wiped out in the 'Great War'.

Flanked by twin towers, this dazzling white statue now presides over neat meadows, grazed by sheep. It takes an enormous effort to imagine the conditions faced here by the combatants of 1917; a moonscape of sucking quagmire, pervasive damp, the foetid stench of rotting bodies, incessant fatigue and the pendulum swing between gut-wrenching fear and mind-numbing routine. For the millions who died, such was their last wretched experience. Those that lived were scarred for life.

History is damning in its indictment of those responsible. From today's standpoint, the sacrifices of that war have no obvious redeeming aspect. There was no tyranny or oppression to extinguish, no clash of ideologies. Accusations of aggression can be levelled at a number of its principal protagonists. It seems the inflated pride of Europe sucked its citizens into a war perpetuated largely for its own sake.

That perspective persists in the enduring view of the war's operational conduct. The belief is that methods were outmoded, ill considered and reprehensible in their cost to human life. Commanders on all sides now stand accused of cowardice and murder; 'donkeys', 'butchers', and 'bunglers' are but a few of the contemptuous terms directed at them. Whilst there are compelling arguments to support a damning view of the causes of conflict, to carry that seam of logic onto the battlefield is overly dismissive, especially if harnessing hindsight to do so. When analysing conflict, the true face of war must not be forgotten but relativism does the dead no justice.

In reality, there were both commanders who failed to grasp the revolutionary developments in warfare and those who kept pace, thinking laterally and incorporating successful ideas into doctrine. The celebration of the latter is sometimes as one-dimensional as the vilification of the former. Much lauded is the German use of highly trained shock troops during offensives at Caporetto in November 1917 and on the Western Front in March 1918, or the British Expeditionary Force (BEF) at Cambrai making spectacular gains using tanks in November 1917.

However, ultimately, even in those instances, it was neither solely a novel tactic nor wonder weapon that prevailed. As is most often the case in military operations, success was found in the application of experience and innovation to the disciplines of exhaustive planning and meticulous preparation. In this equation too, Mother Canada has relevance because the battle in April 1917 for the place where she now stands is a shining example. Nowhere is the accusation of *universal* military incompetence better rebuffed.

# VIMY RIDGE AND THE PURSUIT OF BREAKTHROUGH

From the west, Vimy Ridge is not a hugely imposing feature as its gradient is surprisingly gentle. However, in a war dominated by the primacy of the defensive, it was a vital feature for in other directions it overlooks a large swathe of northern France. To its north-east lie the coalfields of Lens and Douai, crucial to any industrial war effort, to its south the mercantile city of Arras and the open Scarpe River valley.

This significance was realized as early as 1914, when the advancing Germans snatched it as a priority. Thereafter, the French paid dearly in their repeated attempts to recapture it during the Artois offensive of 1915. For a short time, they succeeded but whereas they managed to consolidate the equally pronounced Lorette Spur beyond Souchez to the north-west, they could not hold the crest of Vimy Ridge against the concerted counter-attacks of Kronprinz Rupprecht's Bavarian Army Group. The enterprise cost the French nation 150,000 casualties.

1916 brought renewed determination, 'a heating of national temper among the chief belligerents' as Captain Cyril Falls puts it in the official British history. The men who had volunteered in droves at the war's outset were now ready for battle. Initial procurement orders had materialised and seemingly valuable lessons had been drawn from the 1915 offensives. The line was rebalanced to accommodate the burgeoning BEF and release French divisions for offensive action. In March 1916, the British took over the trenches at Vimy Ridge.

Unexpectedly, French plans were pre-empted by the German offensive at Verdun, which became a bloody, obstinate affair that went on to consume nearly half a million lives.

Desperate, the French implored the British to relieve the pressure with an offensive of their own. The result was the infamous battle of the Somme. Planners put their faith in the destructive potential of massed artillery. Although the requirement to protect assaulting infantry was identified, it was not delivered because of the inaccuracy and impotency of the artillery deployed.

It was costly for Germany too. Their German intolerance of any territorial retirement compelled them to answer all Entente gains, no matter how insignificant, with counter-attacks. The resultant casualties at both Verdun and the Somme were irreplaceable. By the year's end it was clear something would have to give.

This fact was not lost on the French and British planners. Despite the alarming losses of 1916, they believed that a properly co-ordinated joint offensive could shatter the German line. In their enthusiasm the French dubbed this '*à l'outrance*' meaning 'to the death'. In November 1916, an Entente conference was held in Chantilly that laid the foundations of the new offensive; but it was not until the New Year that anything specific was tabled. This was, in part, down to the change of command of French forces that occurred in December. General Joffre was stripped of operational command and given a figurehead role as 'technical adviser' to General Robert Nivelle, who took his place at the head of the Field Armies. Relatively inexperienced, Nivelle was the architect of favourable counter-attacks at Verdun. His supreme confidence bordered on the arrogant and he believed his mastery of artillery could unlock German defences wherever he chose.

## PLANS FOR 1917

The initial intention was to place the BEF under French Command but its commander, Field Marshal Sir Douglas Haig, was vehemently opposed to this – not least because he disagreed with the French over the targets of any future offensives. He wanted to focus his efforts to liberate the Belgian channel ports of Zeebrugge and Ostend as this would put pressure on German submarine operations. Nivelle favoured a more conservative solution. His goal was the destruction of the main body of German forces on the Western Front. The offensive was to be directed in three areas and in three overlapping phases. Two preliminary offensives would be conducted to draw in German reserves, the first by the French *Groupe des Armées du Nord* between the Oise and St Quentin and the second by the BEF between Bapaume and Arras astride the Scarpe River valley. The main thrust by the *Groupe des Armées de Reserve* was to be directed between Reims and Vailly-sur-Aisne focusing on the Chemin des Dames heights that dominated the area. A breakthrough there would permit exploiting formations to roll up the entire German line to the Flemish coast. They

Kaiser Wilhelm (centre) confers with von Hindenburg (left) and Ludendorff (right). Their decision to withdraw to the *Siegfried Stellung* – or Hindenburg Line – was a cleverly calculated expedient. It saved them valuable manpower and complicated Nivelle's offensive plans. (IWM, Q23746)

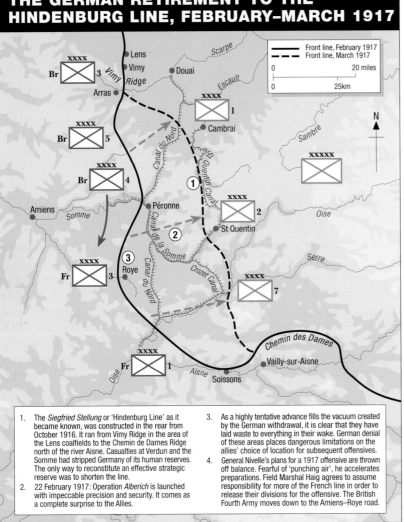

# THE GERMAN RETIREMENT TO THE HINDENBURG LINE, FEBRUARY–MARCH 1917

Front line, February 1917
Front line, March 1917

0        20 miles
0        25km

1. The *Siegfried Stellung* or 'Hindenburg Line' as it became known, was constructed in the rear from October 1916. It ran from Vimy Ridge in the area of the Lens coalfields to the Chemin des Dames Ridge north of the river Aisne. Casualties at Verdun and the Somme had stripped Germany of its human reserves. The only way to reconstitute an effective strategic reserve was to shorten the line.

2. 22 February 1917: Operation *Alberich* is launched with impeccable precision and security. It comes as a complete surprise to the Allies.

3. As a highly tentative advance fills the vacuum created by the German withdrawal, it is clear that they have laid waste to everything in their wake. German denial of these areas places dangerous limitations on the allies' choice of location for subsequent offensives.

4. General Nivelle's plans for a 1917 offensive are thrown off balance. Fearful of 'punching air', he accelerates preparations. Field Marshal Haig agrees to assume responsibility for more of the French line in order to release their divisions for the offensive. The British Fourth Army moves down to the Amiens–Roye road.

would destroy reserves drawn in and pinned by the two preliminary offensives, cut German lines of communication and force them to choose between withdrawal and open battle in decidedly unfavourable circumstances.

It was an audacious plan but not altogether well resourced. French troop shortages after Verdun forced them to relinquish a further 20 miles of front to the BEF in order to muster the divisions required for the spring offensive. Accordingly, General Sir Henry Rawlinson's Fourth Army extended their line south towards Roye but the disposition complicated Haig's planning for the Arras operation and put enormous pressure on his logistic rail infrastructure.

Haig addressed these issues with Nivelle under the Calais Agreement of February 1917. He confirmed command independence for the BEF and was allocated more rail resources. In return, Haig endorsed Nivelle's plan, but yet more consultation was not his priority. He was anxious to get settled and maintain pressure on the Germans, who were contending with desperate manpower shortages of their own. He feared their imminent withdrawal, which if implemented in time, could throw the Allied offensive off balance.

# WITHDRAWAL TO THE HINDENBURG LINE

Planning for the German withdrawal of 1917 had begun the previous year. Irrespective of the careful justifications presented by the German commanders General Paul von Hindenburg and General Erich Ludendorff, ultimately it was a measure born of necessity. The policy of strategic defence in the west, adopted in the wake of their failure in 1914, had handed the initiative to the Allied powers. The absolute refusal to accept any territorial losses in the face of sustained offensives throughout 1915 and 1916 had come at a high price. Extravagant counter-attacks on the Somme and the supposedly limited offensive at Verdun had cost the Germans nearly 750,000 men. With gathering alarm and despondency, they watched the Entente powers draw on the reserves of Empire to expand their armies. Conversely, Germany's dwindling and blockaded population was unable to replace the dead.

As the front line creaked under the strain, German planners considered a fresh belt of defences as an insurance policy. Suitable ground was identified to the rear and preparations commenced in October 1916. Dubbed the *Siegfried Stellung* by the Germans and the 'Hindenburg Line' by the Allies, the new positions ran from Vimy Ridge down to the river Aisne west of the Chemin des Dames. Designed in the context of the latest German defensive doctrine and to a common standard the envy of any soldier on the Western Front, the temptation to utilize the new positions grew stronger as the formidable fortifications began to take shape. The arithmetic alone was seductive to German High Command. A retirement would save 25 miles of front. In manning terms, this amounted to 13 divisions of infantry; precisely the number they needed to create a viable theatre reserve.

**Belts of barbed wire on the Hindenburg Line. The trucks on the horizon betray the scale of the obstacle. German wire had 16 barbs to the foot. Without extensive artillery preparation, wire this thick would even hinder a tank. (IWM, CO 3392)**

General Ludendorff had already halved the establishment of an infantry division in order to create new ones. The only remaining option was an ordered withdrawal to a narrower front that could be defended by fewer men. Preparations were finalized in secrecy, and, on 22 February 1917, Operation *Alberich* was launched. The retreating Germans destroyed everything of any conceivable value to the Allied armies and achieved total surprise.

## THE ARRAS OFFENSIVE TAKES SHAPE

At a stroke, this withdrawal gave credence to the British and French exponents of attrition warfare. It was clear to them that the Germans were being worn down. Certainly, jubilation at the bloodless advance into a vacuum had to be tempered by the understanding that it had already been paid for by hundreds of thousands of men on the Somme, at Verdun and elsewhere.

Haig's fears were in danger of being realised. The vacated ground was wholly unsuited to subsequent offensive operations against the Hindenburg Line. Consequently, the attack between the Oise and St Quentin by the French *Groupe des Armées du Nord* under General Franchet d'Espérey was no longer viable as a major offensive. It was reduced in scope and scale to the status of a 'diversion'.

Nivelle pressed ahead with his plans for a full-scale offensive by General Alfred Micheler's *Groupe des Armées de Reserve* on the Chemin des Dames, as this part of the front line had not changed shape. Similarly, Haig's Arras offensive was fixed on the northern extremity of the Hindenburg Line and therefore was still feasible. They agreed on a timetable culminating in early April.

Haig built his plans around General Sir Edmund Allenby's Third Army, focused on the Scarpe River valley east of Arras. The low-lying

**An 18-pdr. gun battery moving along the St Pol–Arras road in February 1917. Preparations for the Arras offensive began in late 1916 but the BEF commander, Field Marshal Haig, was compelled to revisit them in view of the German withdrawal to the Hindenburg Line. (IWM, Q4684)**

ground was conducive to attack on a broad front. XVIII, VI and VII Corps of that army were earmarked accordingly. Roughly a third of the attacking battalions in those corps heralded from Scotland, the remainder being largely English.

To reinforce the open southern flank, General Sir Hubert Gough's Fifth Army would attack at Bullecourt with its I Australian and New Zealand Army Corps (ANZAC).

When drafting the Calais Agreement, Haig had been compelled to justify his decision to attack Vimy Ridge on the northern flank. Nivelle considered it impregnable and thought any operation against it to be a waste of manpower. Haig disagreed. Its defenders would be able to observe the Scarpe Valley and influence the key battle there. He considered it vital.

Therefore he planned a deliberate *supporting* attack, limited to the capture of Vimy Ridge. This he entrusted to General Sir Henry Horne's First Army. It was to be the hinge on which the entire Arras offensive would swing. Horne was fortunate in being able to marshal the efforts of an entire army onto a five mile front, giving him decisive advantages in artillery. Of his three corps, he selected the newly formed Canadians for the assault, bolstering them with the British 5th Division from XI Corps. The line ot the north was held by I Corps and the balance of XI Corps.

For their part, the Germans knew what was coming. Two-and-a-half years of war had identified those locations where offensives were attractive, while the withdrawal to the Hindenburg Line had served to restrict the options for the Allies even more. There was nothing left to do except rely on the new defensive system to resist.

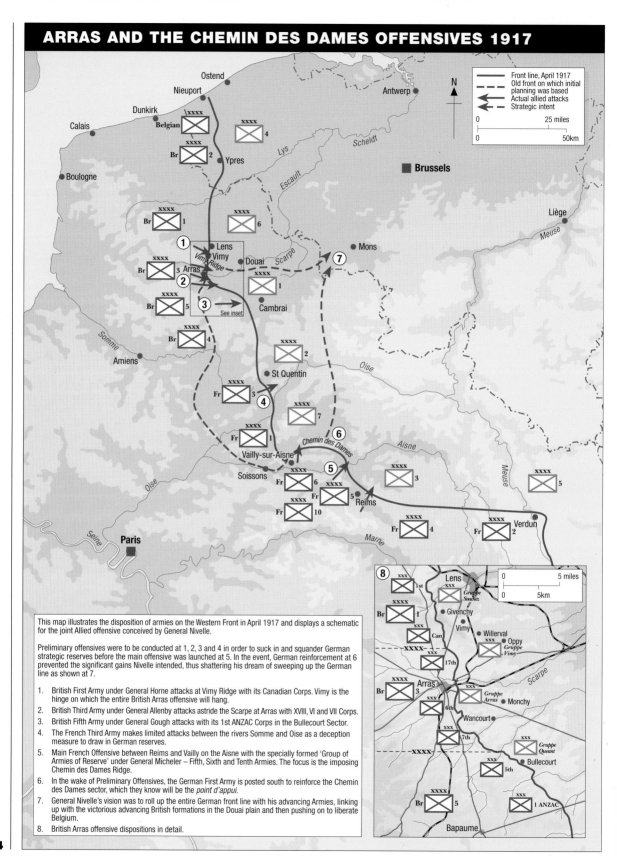

Front line, April 1917
Old front on which initial planning was based
Actual allied attacks
Strategic intent

0 — 25 miles
0 — 50km

N

This map illustrates the disposition of armies on the Western Front in April 1917 and displays a schematic for the joint Allied offensive conceived by General Nivelle.

Preliminary offensives were to be conducted at 1, 2, 3 and 4 in order to suck in and squander German strategic reserves before the main offensive was launched at 5. In the event, German reinforcement at 6 prevented the significant gains Nivelle intended, thus shattering his dream of sweeping up the German line as shown at 7.

1.  British First Army under General Horne attacks at Vimy Ridge with its Canadian Corps. Vimy is the hinge on which the entire British Arras offensive will hang.

2.  British Third Army under General Allenby attacks astride the Scarpe at Arras with XVIII, VI and VII Corps.

3.  British Fifth Army under General Gough attacks with its 1st ANZAC Corps in the Bullecourt Sector.

4.  The French Third Army makes limited attacks between the rivers Somme and Oise as a deception measure to draw in German reserves.

5.  Main French Offensive between Reims and Vailly on the Aisne with the specially formed 'Group of Armies of Reserve' under General Micheler – Fifth, Sixth and Tenth Armies. The focus is the imposing Chemin des Dames Ridge.

6.  In the wake of Preliminary Offensives, the German First Army is posted south to reinforce the Chemin des Dames sector, which they know will be the *point d'appui*.

7.  General Nivelle's vision was to roll up the entire German front line with his advancing Armies, linking up with the victorious advancing British formations in the Douai plain and then pushing on to liberate Belgium.

8.  British Arras offensive dispositions in detail.

# CHRONOLOGY

## 1914

**4 August** – Start of World War I

**August** – Battles of Mons, Ardennes and Le Cateau as the BEF and French try to stem the German advance into Belgium and France

**September** – Allied counter-attacks on the Marne, Artois and Aisne drive the Germans back

**October** – The struggle for manoeuvre culminates in the battle for the Flemish town of Ypres. The hasty defences from Switzerland to the Channel ports solidify through the winter

## 1915

**March** – British offensive at Neuve Chapelle. Failure attributed to 'poor communication'

**April** – Germans initiate second battle of Ypres. Poisonous gas used for the first time

**May to October** – Second Battle of Artois. French attempt to capture Vimy Ridge and the Lorette Spur. Gains include the Lorette Spur and a toehold on the ridge but Germans remain in control

**September to October** – British attack at Loos. First use of the 'creeping barrage'

## 1916

**February** – Germans attack the French at Verdun

**July** – British offensive on the Somme opens in response

**November** – Battle of Somme concluded. Gains of just seven miles no consolation for 500,000 casualties. Germans lose 420,000. Chantilly Conference between Entente powers discusses options for the New Year

**October to December** – Battle of Verdun ends with neither side having gained a territorial advantage. Casualties equal on both sides at a total of 700,000

## 1917

**February** – Calais Agreement between Britain and France sets arrangements for the joint spring offensive. Germans achieve strategic surprise with Operation *Alberich* – the retreat to the Hindenburg Line

**March** – Arras offensive confirmed and preparations are hastened

**20 March** – British bombardment of Vimy Ridge opens

**5 April** – Final preparatory phase of bombardment

**6 April** – America enters the war

**9 April** – British Arras offensive is launched. Startling gains made astride the river Scarpe. Southern half of Vimy Ridge captured in a single bound. Northern end of Vimy Ridge (Hill 145) remains in German hands

**10 April** – Hill 145 captured by Canadians. Further gains made on the river Scarpe but momentum already dissipating

**11 April** – ANZACs attack at Bullecourt on the extreme south of the Arras front. Only limited gains achieved

**12 April** – 'The Pimple' and Bois-en-Hache captured at northern end of Arras front. Elsewhere, offensive slows considerably

**13 April** – Germans withdraw to their reserve lines, conceding terrain in favour of respite. French preliminary offensive opens at St Quentin

**15 April** – British call a pause to the Arras offensive

**16 April** – French launch the assault on Chemin des Dames. Despite encouraging early signs, heavy losses are inflicted and no breakthrough is apparent

**23 April to 24 May** – Limited British attacks across the Arras front aimed at maintaining pressure and shaping the line

**5 May** – Chemin des Dames concluded at no demonstrable strategic gain. French 'mutiny' arises

**7 June** – British assault Messines Ridge south of Ypres after detonation of 19 massive mines

**July to November** – Third battle of Ypres (Passchendaele) launched. The muddy impasse costs Britain 400,000 casualties and Germany 348,000

**20 November** – British attack towards Cambrai using massed tanks for the first time. Gains of five miles are not exploited because of unreliability of the tanks and insufficient reserves. German counter-attacks recapture most of the ground by December

# 1918

**March** – Germans open their offensive on the Somme, making huge gains but exhausting their logistic capabilities

**April** – German subsidiary offensive in Flanders fails as the buttress of Ypres holds firm

**May** – After a diversionary attack west of the Chemin des Dames, Germany launches its final offensive at the French between Soissons and Reims. The biggest advances since 1914 see the Germans pressing against the Marne again but the overextended forces are checked with the assistance of fresh US divisions

**June to July** – Further German offensives lack the impetus of early efforts and result in withdrawals

**August** – The Allied counter-attacks commence across the entire front. Spent German forces are forced into full retreat

**September** – Germans have been driven back to their start point on the Hindenburg Line by the end of the month. US forces make significant gains south-east of Verdun. Further offensives planned for the end of the month

**October** – BEF, French and US forces press home co-ordinated offensives across the entire Western Front, breaching German defensive lines routinely. The British First Army reaches Mons

**11 November** – Armistice is signed and the Germans agree to pull back east of the Rhine within 14 days

# OPPOSING COMMANDERS

## LIMITATIONS OF A MILITARY REVOLUTION

The decades either side of World War I display some of the most alarming social and technological advances in human history. From the military perspective, the pace of this transition is truly remarkable. The senior commanders of the war started their professional careers in regiments that were virtually indistinguishable from those that fought in the Crimea. In the early 1880s, the British Army still used single-shot weapons and wore red tunics in the field. Tactical emphasis remained on moving from column into line. Breech-loading artillery was only just coming into service.

By 1917 those *same men* were commanding formations that utilised combat and reconnaissance aircraft, aerial photography, massed quick-firing indirect artillery, chemical weapons, machine guns, tanks, motorized logistic assets, and reinforced concrete fortification. Their troops would have more in common with the experience of today's soldier than a man who fought in the Zulu War just 30 years previously. The pace at which these men had to assimilate change is unprecedented in military history. Their aptitude for meeting and managing that change has come to be the main criteria they are judged against.

The challenge was not just conceptual. Often they knew what was required but were unable to deliver it. World War I is unique in the singular disparity between weapons and communications technology. Only in the understanding of this challenge can the leadership of World War I commanders be appraised fairly.

Commanders can only influence events if informed of developments in time to react with their decisions. That is the essence of battlefield communication. Telegraph and field telephones enabled static positions to communicate (though the accompanying infrastructure was vulnerable) but radios were in their infancy and too cumbersome for battlefield use. Troops in the assault were forced to rely on runners, whistles, bugles and even carrier pigeons to convey their message. Once battle was joined, the field commander had no better means of influencing events than his Napoleonic or even medieval forebears. Moreover, unlike earlier wars, they could not see the battle unfolding with their own eyes.

Even in normal daily life, our reaction to the absence of communication is to make plans and stick to them. This is what a general in World War I was compelled to do – hence the rigidity so apparent in his approach. Nor was this limited to the senior level; battalion and brigade commanders faced the same difficulty. Hence we have the curious contradiction of a highly centralised planning process, normally at the corps or divisional level, decentralised down to the company or even platoon level once battle was joined.

Clearly, there is a degree to which this argument has been oversimplified. Of course brigade and battalion commanders were able to influence their own plans to a degree but one imposing characteristic of battles in this period was the *interdependence* of effort. This was a symptom of the desperate limitations placed on manoeuvre by the linear nature of the battlefield. Moreover, senior commanders, culturally averse to relinquishing all responsibility for an offensive, were often prescriptive beyond necessity.

Squeezed into predictable avenues of attack and unable to influence the battle decisively except by adept planning, the better commanders in World War I stood out by virtue of their ability to innovate and keep pace with technological changes.

# THE GERMANS

Arguably, German commanders were the quickest to adjust to the new way of war. The hideous losses inflicted in 1914 had effaced their tactical naivety and triggered a rapid reassessment. The High Command concluded that a defensive mindset was the best option for securing the Western Front until they had subdued Russia.

Superb engineers, they mastered the art of constructing virtually impregnable defensive positions and were responsible for the key invention of reinforced concrete. Pre-war emphasis on highly efficient staff officers driving the planning process was also a characteristic that suited the deliberate and logistically demanding nature of operations.

The battle for Vimy Ridge was influenced by a number of different German command levels. Generals Ludendorff and von Hindenburg were responsible for the defensive system adopted by the German army in 1917. The Army Group around Arras was commanded by the experienced figure of Kronprinz (Crown Prince) Rupprecht of Bavaria, who had commanded the Sixth Army, capturing Vimy Ridge in the Schlieffen offensive of 1914. His high rank does not allude to nepotism as his promotion to Army Group command in 1916 had been on the basis of merit.

Kronprinz Rupprecht of Bavaria, Army Group commander for the northern half of the Western Front. In 1914, Bavaria was still an autonomous kingdom and its armies marched under their own flag. (IWM, Q45320)

### Colonel-General Freiherr von Falkenhausen
The defenders of Vimy Ridge came under the command of the German Sixth Army, led by Colonel-General Freiherr von Falkenhausen. At 73 years old, he was a Bavarian of the old school who had handled his Sixth Army at the Somme with tenacity. It gave him enormous confidence in the methods of German defence. He favoured the *Gruppe* system of battlefield command whereby corps headquarters formed the basis of flexible formations, organised and resourced as necessary to achieve efficiency. He had four such configurations at the Battle of Arras – *Gruppen Loos, Souchez, Vimy* and *Arras*. If the enemy attacked at the boundary between two *Gruppen*, neighbouring units would be switched to one or the other by mutual accord.

### General of Infantry Karl Ritter von Fasbender
In command of *Gruppe Vimy* was the 65-year-old General of Infantry Karl von Fasbender. In effect, he was in control of the ridge, though the northern extremity came under *Gruppe Souchez*. Von Fasbender was

Lieutenant-General the Hon Sir Julian Byng, GOC Canadian Corps. He looks stern in this photograph but he was noted for his approachability and harboured great affection for his men. As a young officer, he entertained peers and troops alike with his banjo. (IWM, CO 1369)

another highly experienced Bavarian who on the official order of battle commanded the 1st Bavarian Reserve Corps. A reservist himself, he had been called out of retirement in 1914 to command the corps having served with distinction right back to the Franco-Prussian war. His investiture as a Knight of the Military Order of Max Joseph for his leadership in the fluid battles of 1914 and award of the *Pour le Mérite* for his part in the Somme confirms his status as a distinguished commander.

# THE BRITISH AND CANADIANS

British generalship in World War I is one of the most keenly debated topics in modern military history. A section of this brevity precludes any significant re-appraisal but unquestionably, Germany's occupation of France and Belgium compelled both the French and BEF to take the initiative and this compounded the operational challenges already discussed.

In attempting to eject Germany's forces from their elaborate defences, the emphasis for the BEF had to lie with infantry assault. This is as true today as it was then. As has been proved time and again, only infantry in close-quarters combat are able to take and hold ground comprehensively. The challenge faced by offensive planners was how to protect that infantry in the assault – by both direct and indirect means. In the operation to capture Vimy Ridge, this remained the chief preoccupation.

### General Sir Henry Horne

General Sir Henry Horne was in command of the First Army. A Royal Horse Artilleryman, he had been promoted from the post of Chief of Royal Artillery in the BEF. Small in stature, particular and decorous, Horne was a cautious commander. Having selected the Canadian Corps to attack Vimy Ridge, Horne was comfortable in letting its commander Lieutenant-General the Honourable Sir Julian Byng pursue the detail. Nevertheless, his contribution to the battle is often overlooked, even though he supervised the planning process and was instrumental in managing the attachment of army level resources.

### Lieutenant-General the Honourable Sir Julian Byng

The seventh son of the Earl of Strafford, Byng had been commissioned into the 10th Hussars in 1882, serving first in Sudan against the Mahdi and then in command of irregular cavalry during the South African war at the turn of the century. Appointed General Officer Commanding British Forces Egypt before the war, he went on to command the 3rd Cavalry Division in the campaigns of 1914.

In 1915 he was promoted to command of IX Corps and deployed to the Dardanelles just in time to help effect the miraculously bloodless evacuation operation for which he was awarded the KBE (Knight of the British Empire). 1916 saw him posted to the Canadian Corps aged 54.

Conspicuously caring and approachable, Byng belies the stereotype of the World War I British general. With charisma and imagination, he soon stamped his mark on the Canadian Corps as a confident and innovative commander with a ruthless eye for detail. It was a highly successful match.

# OPPOSING ARMIES

## THE GERMAN ARMY AT VIMY RIDGE

**A**s has been described, *Gruppe Vimy* was effectively an ad hoc formation based around the 1st Bavarian Army Corps under the command of General of Infantry Karl von Fasbender. A German army corps comprised of four divisions, each of which was their basic independent manoeuvre element at that time. Established strength of a division was in the region of 13,000 men. The four divisions in *Gruppe Vimy* were the 1st Bavarian Reserve Infantry Division, 79th Reserve Infantry Division (Prussian), 14th Bavarian Infantry Division and the 18th Bavarian Infantry Division, though the latter was detached and held in the Sixth Army reserve under the control of Colonel-General von Falkenhausen.

British First Army objectives on Vimy Ridge did not square off neatly against *Gruppe Vimy*. Their southernmost formation, 14th Bavarian Infantry Division, held the area above the river Scarpe and fought Third Army's XVII Corps. The 1st Bavarian Infantry Division occupied the lower reaches of Vimy Ridge and so straddled the boundary between the Canadian Corps and XVII Corps' 51st Division. Only one of its regiments fought the Canadians. A division of *Gruppe Souchez* – the 16th Bavarian Infantry Division, held the area above Givenchy at the northern end of the ridge. Their 11th Infantry Regiment overlapped the Canadian Corps' objectives and aided *Gruppe Vimy's* defence.

*Gruppe Souchez* was under the command of General of Infantry Wichura and his 8th Reserve Corps headquarters. Other divisions in that group were 56th Infantry Division and 80th Reserve Division but they played only a battalion-level reinforcing role in the battle.

A German reserve *Stellung* on the Somme. It might appear to be in poor repair but the bunker and dugout are looking solid enough. Note all the field telephone cable. (IWM, Q23931)

A German Maxim team in action in February 1917. This position is ad hoc by Teutonic standards but given the wholesale destruction of their fighting positions at Vimy, it is a more reliable illustration of the way the nests would have looked. Note the 'sledge' mount, which alone weighed 83lb. (IWM, Q44170)

In 1917, each infantry division fielded three regiments, notionally within a brigade.[1] Details of the specific regiments in the divisions of *Gruppe Vimy* can be found in the order of battle section. In strength, each regiment equated roughly to a British brigade in that it contained three battalions.

The line held by a division was split up into regimental frontages of approximately 1,000m. Each regimental sector was responsible for manning its own depth back to the rear areas. This was achieved by rotating the three battalions through one of three duties. One battalion held the frontline positions – normally at least two parallel fire trenches known as the *I Stellung*. The second battalion was situated in like manner on the support line (or *II Stellung*) to the immediate rear. Distances varied but generally it was about 1km or more behind. The third battalion was placed 'at rest' up to 6km to the rear and beyond the range of most enemy artillery. In the event of attack, the reserve battalion was earmarked for counter-attack or manning of third line (*III Stellung*) reserve positions nearest their billets. The term 'at rest' is placed in inverted commas because usually it was anything but.

At Vimy Ridge, defences were thickened by the addition of another support trench system between *I* and *II Stellung*, dubbed the *Zwischenstellung* – 'intermediate position'. Therefore, the *II Stellung* to the east of the ridge became the regimental reserve line manned by resting battalions and the *III Stellung* (known to the British as the Oppy–Mericourt Line) in the middle of the Douai plain was set aside for reserve divisions under Sixth Army control.

In terms of garrisoning the line itself, battalion sectors would be sub-divided into four company areas, two abreast holding the leading trench or, and the other two to the rear in mutual support. This point is important because often you see maps denoting a regiment in the front line when in reality, that piece of ground was only occupied by a battalion. It can be misleading.

The rifle company was, by establishment, 264 men strong but by 1917 the actual number was significantly less. Undermanning was caused by conscription and training shortfalls (increasingly acute as the war progressed) as well as casualties inflicted by the enemy. Sickness and accident also took their toll, with many men carried on establishment

A German 10.5cm light field howitzer in an emplacement. This workhorse of the German field artillery could hurl a 33lb shell up to 6,000m. Each infantry division was equipped with 12. (IWM, Q23721)

but unfit for frontline duty and only suitable for administrative fatigues under the quartermasters.

On Vimy Ridge the rifle companies numbered about 150 men at most. When the Canadian Corps attacked on 9 April, each company frontage faced two or more battalions of infantry of up to 1,000 men each. These drastic odds were levelled by an intelligent system of defence. Planners incorporated deep dugouts, carefully sited concrete strongpoints and barbed wire entanglements with a deadly web of interlocking or overlapping machine-gun arcs.

At the time the Germans were using the 1908-pattern water-cooled Maxim machine gun. Some have claimed that it killed more people than any other single weapon since the Roman short sword. Weighing 120lb with its sledge mount, it was heavy and cumbersome but incredibly reliable and well suited to the static role in which it was employed. Its cyclic rate of fire was slow by modern standards – about 400–500 rounds a minute – but economical as a consequence.[2] In 1917, each battalion had a machine-gun company with eight guns, mainly in the second line. Machine guns are at their most murderous at greater distances as the rounds have time to spread out and form what is termed a 'beaten zone' if they impact or a 'cone of fire' in flight.

As the war progressed, infantry divisions formed unofficial specialist machine-gun detachments manned by selected marksmen and formed into companies of a dozen guns. These were used to hold the vital concrete strongpoints designed to sustain resistance when bypassed or overrun by the enemy.

In addition to the heavy Maxims, each company was scaled for six Maxim 08/15 light machine guns. At 50lb apiece, these were still less than half the weight of a normal Maxim. Their relative mobility made them vital assets for counter-attacks and reinforcement of exposed frontline outposts. In reality, a company was lucky if it mustered three 08/15s.

As demonstrated at Beaumont Hamel on the first day of the Somme, a well-sited machine gun could decimate an entire battalion and the Germans put a great deal of thought into their disposition. The effect of a weapon could also be multiplied by the use of slanting as opposed to linear wire belts, which channelled the enemy into pre-determined 'killing areas'. The 1,000m range of machine guns also allowed them to support other sectors on the frontage that might be struggling to hold the line.

Mortar and artillery resources provided indirect fire support. Alongside the machine gun, this was the most effective means of defeating an attack. Taken as a whole, indirect fire killed more men than gas, machine guns, or rifle fire but this statistic is distorted by the fact that indirect weapons were in use all the time in a harassing role.

Each battalion had six 7.6cm mortars (known as *Minenwerfer*) grouped as a company and dug into their own emplacements. These were muzzle-loaded, high-trajectory weapons that lobbed high-explosive shells over a relatively short range. They were useful for harassing fire as well as delivery of smoke to screen raids but were best employed as part of a co-ordinated, pre-agreed fire plan in response to attack.

The division's three batteries of 7.7cm field guns and three batteries of 10.5cm field howitzers delivered heavier firepower.[3] Each battery contained four artillery pieces and they would be positioned well to the rear, out of view. Again, their fire was largely pre-planned and could be initiated by coloured signal rocket if field telephone communications broke down. All indirect fire weapons are at their most efficient against closely packed troops in the open, especially in the first few seconds before those men take cover. This fact was not lost on the Germans and the gunners were the first people a company headquarters would alert if attacked. Larger calibre artillery was available at the army group or corps level and would be tasked according to priorities laid down by von Fasbender.

A pioneer battalion supported each division. Its two field companies were dedicated to menial engineering tasks and repair work with assistance from battalions in 'rest'. German battalions changed over less regularly than their British counterparts and in some cases spent weeks rather than days in the front line before moving back. In light of their defensive

**Bavarian prisoners of war captured on Vimy Ridge. The Bavarians were excellent soldiers and among the most dependable the Kaiser could muster. The swelling on the left POW's cheek could be an abscess or a souvenir of Canadian hospitality at point of capture. (IWM, CO 1225)**

mindset, the Germans had gone to great lengths to make themselves at home on the ridge and certainly invested time and effort in creating deep dugouts to shelter in. The chalk at Vimy is perfect for this work as it is soft enough to mine but hard enough to withstand shelling.

The most elaborate system of dugouts was the *Hangstellung* – slope position – under the steeper eastern lee of Vimy Ridge. Not only was it impervious to even the heaviest shelling but its inhabitants had made it *relatively* comfortable. Victorious attackers were always surprised to find such incongruous items as kitchen dressers, iron beds and even carpet.

One should not be confused as to the true character of life on Vimy Ridge however. German troops have always been noted for their rugged stoicism and this episode was no exception. The air down in those dugouts was foul. Everything was damp. When it rained on the surface, a few days later it would 'rain' in the tunnels and dugouts as well. They were infested with enormous rats that scuttled and scavenged fearlessly. The claustrophobia when under barrage can only be imagined and eyewitness accounts abound with instances of men going berserk. Up in the trenches, it was little better. They were frozen, flooded, muddy or dusty as the season dictated. Constantly harassed by sniping, raids and shellfire, the men either developed the survival senses of a wild animal or became casualties.

The work required to maintain these defences was a Herculean labour and hazardous with it. Rations were meagre, only rarely included meat and more often than not, arrived cold and congealed. When not ersatz, coffee and tobacco – the staple of any German soldier – was in short supply.

In spite of all this, the Bavarians sang their rousing mountain songs and carved little wooden mementoes from the timbers. They were the flower of the German army, courageous, stolid, dependable and proficient. The Prussians in the 79th Division were also a respected breed. Relatively new to the Western Front, they had proved themselves against the Russians in the East. Now they would face the Canadian Corps.

# THE CANADIAN CORPS AT VIMY RIDGE

A great deal has been written about the Canadian Corps at Vimy Ridge. Most histories, particularly those emanating from Canada, fail to acknowledge that it was an army level, British operation. Some even claim that the British failed to take the ridge before the Canadians arrived when it is clear that no attempt had taken place since the French Artois offensive of 1915.

The Canadian Corps was still part of the British army and a significant number of its staff officers were British, particularly since Canada had a tiny standing professional army at the start of the war. For the operation to capture Vimy Ridge, General Sir Henry Horne attached the entire 5th Division from I Corps, and its 13th Infantry Brigade fought as part of the Canadian 2nd Division. The tunnellers who built the subways and mines were British, as were the heavy gunners attached from I Corps and First Army. This swelled their ranks to 170,000, of which 97,000 were Canadian.

Nevertheless, the Canadian emphasis is understandable. It was the first time they had fought as an independent corps and the victory is a

Canadian troops at rest behind Vimy Ridge. This is a fantastic portrait of the fighting man. Simply delighted to be out of the line, at home mending shirts in a chalky pit and sporting the classic 'face and forearms' tan. The rugged Canadians were natural soldiers. (IWM, CO 1463)

key chapter in the realization of their proud nationhood. Furthermore, their achievements *are* justly celebrated. The so-called 'Dominion' troops – Australians, New Zealanders, South Africans and Canadians – were undoubtedly among the best the BEF could field.

The Canadian expeditionary forces belonged to the bellicose and energetic Sam Hughes, the Minister of Militia. Though combative (eventually being removed from office in December 1916), he was instrumental in ensuring that his Canadians were given the opportunity to fight as a cohesive entity. By and large the men he recruited and sent to France were rugged characters accustomed to a hardy existence. As emigrants or descendents of emigrants, they were enterprising and entrepreneurial men. Of their four divisional commanders, only Major-General Henry Burstall of the 2nd Division was a regular officer. The remainder were militia officers. Major-General David Watson commanding 4th Division was the owner of the *Quebec Chronicle*. The most celebrated of all was Major-General Arthur Currie of the 1st Division, who went on to command the Canadian Corps after Byng's promotion. Before the war he was a real-estate broker. By no means all the Canadians who fought at Vimy were native born. Many had only recently emigrated from the British Isles and certainly did not have the accents we associate with Canada today. In part, this accounts for the alacrity with which so many young Canadian men volunteered in 1914.

The Canadians saw action for the first time in April 1915 at Second Ypres, where their 1st Division held the line against repeated German attacks despite being subjected to the first use of chlorine gas. As more trained volunteers arrived from Canada in 1916, they formed the 2nd and 3rd Divisions, fighting again at Ypres at the battle of St Eloi in April, and then with distinction on the Somme at Courcelette in November 1916.

Canadian infantry marching out of the line past pack mules at Ancre on the Somme in November 1916. The Canadians had already made their name at Second Ypres in 1915 when, without masks or protection of any sort, they stood firm in the face of the first gas attack on the Western Front. They went from strength to strength. (IWM, CO 1007)

In terms of organization, equipment, and doctrine, by 1917 the Canadian Corps was identical to that of any other in the BEF. Held centrally by corps headquarters were the Cavalry Brigade, Engineers and Tunnellers, three brigades of Garrison (Siege) Artillery and two brigades of Field Artillery. There was also the Motor Machine-Gun Brigade with its 38 Vickers guns, similar in weight and performance to the German Maxim. Thereafter, the Corps was sub-divided into five independent, balanced divisions – 1st, 2nd, 3rd and 4th with the 5th British Division attached. The numbering of that British division is entirely coincidental.

A division was built around three infantry brigades, commanded by brigadier-generals. The brigades fielded four infantry battalions with an established strength of just over 1,000 men each, of which about half were in the pure infantry role and the remainder in support functions. A trench mortar company equipped with eight 3in. Stokes mortars provided intrinsic indirect fire support. The brigadier could also call upon his machine-gun company of 16 Vickers.

The division had a considerable amount of indirect firepower at its disposal. Its two field artillery brigades each comprised three batteries of 18-pdr. guns (at six guns per battery) and one battery of six 4.5in. howitzers, a weapon of similar capability. The Commander Royal Artillery in divisional headquarters could also utilize the trench mortar brigade with its three batteries of four 4in. medium mortars and single battery of four 9.45in. heavy mortars. For an attack on the scale of Vimy Ridge, the indirect fire plan was organized at the corps level, with all assets except machine guns massed into a central pool.

Unlike the Germans defending the ridge, Canadian and British units were well manned and went into the attack near enough at full-established strength. The battalion's four rifle companies were further sub-divided into four platoons of 36 men. This was the basic grouping for the assault and the lowest level of command that would be given a specific objective. By 1917, the infantry platoon had taken on the basic shape that endures to this day: four sections with a small headquarters element under a subaltern officer.

From top to bottom, the Canadian Corps was a first class organization amply trained, equipped and motivated for the task ahead.

---

1 This was a throwback to 1914 and 1915 when each division had six regiments in two brigades. In 1916 the infantry strength of divisions was halved to save manpower.
2 This does not mean that it fired that many rounds in so short a timeframe. Belts of ammunition only came in lengths of 250 rounds and it was most efficient in short bursts.
3 The difference between a field gun and field howitzer is that the latter is designed for high-angle shooting and is normally of a slightly higher calibre. By 1917, the distinction was becoming less relevant as gun design started to account for greater elevation.

# ORDERS OF BATTLE

## BRITISH ARMY

**The Canadian Corps** – Lt. Gen. Hon Sir Julian Byng

Corps troops
  Canadian Cavalry Brigade – Brig. Gen. J. E. B. Seely
        Royal Canadian Dragoons (Detached to Third Army)
        Fort Garry Horse (Detached to Third Army)
        Canadian Light Horse

  Artillery – Brig. Gen. E. W. B. Morrison
        Royal Canadian Horse Artillery Brigade
        1st Brigade, Canadian Garrison Artillery
        2nd Brigade, Canadian Garrison Artillery
        3rd Brigade, Canadian Garrison Artillery

  Engineers – Brig. Gen. W. B. Lindsay
        Corps Survey Section
        1st Tramways Company
        2nd Tramways Company
        1st, 2nd, 3rd, 4th Field Engineer Companies
        67th Canadian Pioneer Battalion
        123rd Canadian Pioneer Battalion
        1st, 2nd, 3rd, 4th Canadian Entrenchment Battalions

        Machine guns – Col. R. Brutinel
        1st Motor Machine-Gun Brigade

**1st Division** – Maj. Gen. A. W. Currie
        1st Brigade Canadian Field Artillery
        2nd Brigade Canadian Field Artillery
        1st Brigade Canadian Engineers
        1st Division Ammunition Column
        1st Division Signal Company

        1st Canadian Infantry Brigade – Brig. Gen. W. A. Griesbach
                1st Battalion (Western Ontario)
                2nd Battalion (Eastern Onatario)
                3rd Battalion, Royal Regiment of Canada (Toronto)
                4th Battalion (Western Ontario)
                1st Trench Mortar Battery
                1st Canadian Machine-Gun Company

        2nd Canadian Infantry Brigade – Brig. Gen. F. O. W. Loomis
                5th Battalion (Saskatchewan)
                7th Battalion (British Columbia)
                8th Battalion (Winnipeg) 'The Little Black Devils'
                10th Battalion (Calgary)
                2nd Trench Mortar Battery
                2nd Canadian Machine-Gun Company

        3rd Canadian Infantry Brigade – Brig. Gen. G. S. Tuxford
                13th Battalion, 5th Royal Highlanders (Ontario)
                14th Battalion, The Montreal Regiment (Montreal)
                15th Battalion, 48th Highlanders (Toronto)
                16th Battalion, Canadian Scottish (Vancouver Island)
                3rd Trench Mortar Battery
                3rd Canadian Machine-Gun Company

**2nd Division** – Maj. Gen. H. E. Burstall
        5th Brigade Canadian Field Artillery
        6th Brigade Canadian Field Artillery
        2nd Brigade Canadian Engineers
        2nd Division Ammunition Column
        2nd Division Signal Company
        12 Company, D Battalion, Heavy Machine-Gun Corps (8 x Mk II Tanks)

        4th Canadian Infantry Brigade – Brig. Gen. R. Rennie
                18th Battalion (London Ontario)
                19th Battalion (Central Ontario)
                20th Battalion (Central Ontario)
                21st Battalion (Eastern Ontario)
                4th Trench Mortar Battery
                4th Canadian Machine-Gun Company

        5th Canadian Infantry Brigade – Brig. Gen. A. H. Macdonnell
                22nd Battalion (Canadien Français) 'The Van Doos'
                24th Battalion, Victoria Rifles (Montreal)
                25th Battalion, Novia Scotia Rifles (Novia Scotia)
                26th Battalion (New Brunswick)
                5th Trench Mortar Battery
                5th Canadian Machine-Gun Company

        6th Canadian Infantry Brigade – Brig. Gen. H. B. D. Ketchen
                27th Battalion (Winnipeg)
                28th Battalion (North West Canada)
                29th Battalion (Vancouver) 'Tobin's Tigers'
                31st Battalion (Alberta)
                6th Trench Mortar Battery
                6th Canadian Machine-Gun Company

**3rd Division** – Maj. Gen. L. J. Lipsett
        9th Brigade Canadian Field Artillery
        10th Brigade Canadian Field Artillery
        3rd Brigade Canadian Engineers
        3rd Division Ammunition Column
        3rd Division Signal Company

        7th Canadian Infantry Brigade – Brig. Gen. A. C. Macdonnell
                The Royal Canadian Regiment (Toronto)
                Princess Patricia's Canadian Light Infantry
                42nd Battalion, Royal Highlanders (Montreal) 'The Black Watch'
                49th Battalion (Edmonton)
                7th Trench Mortar Battery
                7th Canadian Machine-Gun Company

        8th Canadian Infantry Brigade – Brig. Gen. J. H. Elmsley
                1st Canadian Mounted Rifles
                2nd Canadian Mounted Rifles
                4th Canadian Mounted Rifles
                5th Canadian Mounted Rifles
                8th Trench Mortar Battery
                8th Canadian Machine-Gun Company

        9th Canadian Infantry Brigade
                43rd Battalion (Winnipeg)
                52nd Battalion (Port Arthur)
                58th Battalion (Brantford)
                116th Battalion (Novia Scotia)
                9th Trench Mortar Battery
                9th Canadian Machine-Gun Company

**4th Division** – Maj. Gen. D. Watson
        3rd Brigade Canadian Field Artillery
        4th Brigade Canadian Field Artillery
        4th Brigade Canadian Engineers
        4th Division Ammunition Column
        4th Division Signal Company

        10th Canadian Infantry Brigade – Brig. Gen. E. Hilliam
                44th Battalion (Winnipeg)
                46th Battalion (Regina and Moose Jaw)
                47th Battalion (British Columbia)
                50th Battalion (Calgary)
                10th Trench Mortar Battery
                10th Canadian Machine-Gun Company

        11th Canadian Infantry Brigade – Brig. Gen. V. W. Odlum
                54th Battalion (Kootenays)
                75th Battalion (Mississauga) 'The Jolly 75'
                87th Battalion, Grenadier Guards (Montreal)
                102nd Battalion (Northern British Columbia) 'Pea-Soupers'
                11th Trench Mortar Battery
                11th Canadian Machine-Gun Company

        12th Canadian Infantry Brigade – Brig. Gen. J. H. MacBrian
                38th Battalion (Ottawa)
                72nd Battalion, Seaforth Highlanders (Vancouver)
                73rd Battalion, Royal Highlanders
                78th Battalion, Winnipeg Grenadiers (Winnipeg)
                85th Battalion, Novia Scotia Highlanders (Novia Scotia)
                12th Trench Mortar Battery
                12th Canadian Machine-Gun Company

### Attached from I Corps

**5th Division** – Maj. Gen. R. B. Stephen
        1st/6th Hussars
        15th Brigade Royal Field Artillery (Attached to 2nd Division)
        27th Brigade Royal Field Artillery (Attached to 2nd Division)
        59th Field Company Royal Engineers
        491st Field Company Royal Engineers
        527th Field Company Royal Engineers
        205th Machine-Gun Company (Attached to 4th Division)
        5th Division Ammunition Column
        5th Division Signal Company

        13th Infantry Brigade – Brig. Gen. L. O. W. Jones (Attached to 2nd Division)
                2nd Battalion, King's Own Scottish Borderers
                1st Battalion, Royal West Kent Regiment
                14th Battalion, Royal Warwickshire Regiment

15th Battalion, Royal Warwickshire Regiment
13th Machine-Gun Company
95th Infantry Brigade – N/K
    1st Battalion, Devonshire Regiment
    1st Battalion, East Surrey Regiment
    1st Battalion, Duke of Cornwall's Light Infantry
    12th Battalion, The Gloucestershire Regiment
    95th Machine-Gun Company

15th Infantry Brigade – Brig. Gen. M. N. Turner
    16th Battalion, Royal Warwickshire Regiment
    1st Battalion, Norfolk Regiment
    1st Battalion, Bedfordshire Regiment
    1st Battalion, Cheshire Regiment
    15th Machine-Gun Company

**Attached from First Army**
Heavy Artillery
    2nd (Canadian) Heavy Artillery Group, Canadian Garrison Artillery (Counter-Battery Group 1)
    50th Heavy Artillery Group, Royal Garrison Artillery (Counter-Battery Group 2)
    76th Heavy Artillery Group, Royal Garrison Artillery (Counter-Battery Group 3)
    11th Heavy Artillery Group, Royal Garrison Artillery (Attached to 1st Division)
    77th Heavy Artillery Group, Royal Garrison Artillery (Attached to 1st Division)
    64th Heavy Artillery Group, Royal Garrison Artillery (Attached to 2nd Division)
    70th Heavy Artillery Group, Royal Garrison Artillery (Attached to 2nd Division)
    13th Heavy Artillery Group, Royal Garrison Artillery (Attached to 3rd Division)
    53rd Heavy Artillery Group, Royal Garrison Artillery (Attached to 3rd Division)
    51st Heavy Artillery Group, Royal Garrison Artillery (Attached to 4th Division)
    1st (Canadian) Heavy Artillery Group, Canadian Garrison Artillery (Attached to 4th Division)

Field Artillery
    31st Division Field Artillery Group (Two Royal Field Artillery brigades)
    63rd Division Field Artillery Group (Two Royal Field Artillery brigades)
    Reserve (Lahore) Field Artillery Group (Two Royal Field Artillery brigades)
    5th Brigade, Royal Horse Artillery
    8th Brigade, Canadian Field Artillery
    18th Brigade, Royal Field Artillery
    26th Brigade, Royal Field Artillery
    28th Brigade, Royal Field Artillery
    76th Brigade, Royal Field Artillery
    93rd Brigade, Royal Field Artillery
    242nd Brigade, Royal Field Artillery

Tunnelling Engineers
    172nd Tunnelling Company Royal Engineers
    176th Tunnelling Company Royal Engineers
    182nd Tunnelling Company Royal Engineers
    185th Tunnelling Company Royal Engineers
    (Approx 500 men each)

**I Corps, 24th Division** – Bois-en-Hache, 12 April 1917

73rd Infantry Brigade – Brig. Gen. W. J. Dugan
    2nd Battalion, The Leinster Regiment
    9th Battalion, Royal Sussex Regiment
    13th Battalion, The Middlesex Regiment
    1st Battalion, Royal Fusiliers
    12th Battalion, Sherwood Foresters (Pioneers)
    73rd Machine-Gun Company
    73rd Trench Mortar Battery

# GERMAN ARMY

**1st Bavarian Reserve Corps** (*Gruppe Vimy*) – General of Infantry Karl von Fasbender

Corps troops
    Artillery
        9th Field Artillery Regiment
        25th Reserve Field Artillery Regiment
        66th Reserve Field Artillery Regiment
        69th Field Artillery Regiment
        Three Batteries of Kriegsmarine 30cm Naval guns

79th Reserve Infantry Division – General of Infantry von Bacmeister
    63rd Reserve Field Artillery Regiment
    Pioneer Battalion
    Cavalry Squadron
    Field Replenishment Depot
    Specialist Machine-Gun Battalion

    261st Reserve Infantry Regiment – Oberst von Goerne
        1st Battalion
        2nd Battalion
        3rd Battalion

    262nd Reserve Infantry Regiment – Major Freiherr von Rotenhan
        1st Battalion
        2nd Battalion
        3rd Battalion

    263rd Reserve Infantry Regiment – Oberstleutnant von Behr
        1st Battalion
        2nd Battalion
        3rd Battalion

Reinforced on 9 April by:
1st Battalion, 118th Reserve Infantry Regiment, 56th Infantry Division
3rd Battalion, 34th Reserve Infantry Regiment, 80th Infantry Division

1st Bavarian Reserve Infantry Division – Generalmajor Freiherr von Bechmann
    3rd Reserve Field Artillery Regiment
    Pioneer Battalion
    Cavalry Squadron
    Field Replenishment Depot
    Specialist Machine-Gun Battalion

    3rd Bavarian Reserve Infantry Regiment – Major Maier
        1st Battalion
        2nd Battalion
        3rd Battalion

Regiment reinforced on 9 April by:
1st Battalion, 225th Infantry Regiment, 17th Division

*Note: 1st Bavarian Reserve Infantry Regiment (Oberstleutnant von Füger), 2nd Bavarian Reserve Infantry Regiment (Oberstleutnant von Brunner) fought the 51st Division of XVII Corps in the Third Army area of operations to the south of Vimy Ridge. They were not involved in the actions described.*

14th Bavarian Infantry Division – General Ritter von Rauchenberger

*Though part of Gruppe Vimy, it took no part in the battle for Vimy Ridge. It was posted on the northern side of the river Scarpe and fought the 34th and 9th Divisions of XVII Corps.*

**8th Reserve Corps** (*Gruppe Souchez*) – General of Infantry Wichura

16th Bavarian Infantry Division – Generalmajor Möhl
    Field Artillery Regiment (Title N/K)
    Pioneer Battalion
    Cavalry Squadron
    Field Replenishment Depot
    Specialist Machine-Gun Battalion

    11th Infantry Regiment – Major Ritter von Braun
        1st Battalion
        2nd Battalion
        3rd Battalion

Regiment reinforced on 10 and 11 April by:
1st Battalion, 14th Bavarian Infantry Regiment (16th Bavarian Infantry Division)
1st Battalion, 21st Bavarian Infantry Regiment (16th Bavarian Infantry Division)
3rd Battalion, 5th Guards Grenadier Regiment (4th Guards Division)
1st Battalion, 93rd Reserve Infantry Regiment (4th Guards Division)

*Note: With the exception of reinforcing battalions specified above, 16th Division's 14th and 21st Bavarian Infantry Regiments remained uncommitted to battle, 56th and 80th Divisions forming the remainder of Gruppe Souchez also only played a reinforcing role.*

# OPPOSING PLANS

## GERMAN PLANS TO DEFEND VIMY RIDGE

A German rifle-grenade emplacement in a wood. This is typical of the positions in the woods on Vimy Ridge just forward of *II Stellung*. (IWM, Q 23932)

I t was not manning pressures alone that drove the Germans to refine their defensive doctrine. The retirement to the Hindenburg Line had been a wise and cleverly executed operation but it was implemented in hand with significant developments in methodology. The fresh fortifications afforded them an opportunity to create a whole new system of defence, deeper and more scientific than the simple approach of placing forces forward in a series of linear positions.

The new doctrine was entitled *Eingreifentaktik* – intervention tactic. Physical defences were to be established in a series of 'zones', thousands of metres apart, sometimes termed 'elastic defence'. The *Vorwärtszone* – forward zone – was nearest to the enemy and consisted of belts of trenches ostensibly in the orthodox model. The key lay in the way they were manned and balanced. Outposts and frontline positions were lightly held and would channel the enemy into a matrix of mutually supporting trenches in the *Widerstand* – resistance line. Concrete strongpoints would hold vital junctions and cover a 360-degree arc, with fighting positions being configured to fire to the rear as well as forward. The entire system was sewn up with thick belts of wire, including 'tangle-foot' beds in low-lying areas.

As a rule, the *Widerstand* was constructed on ground invisible to the enemy until they crested a rise, whereupon they would be ambushed from what is termed a 'reverse slope' position. This is a slope sited on the far side of a valley or depression, beyond the line of sight but too far to rush. Pre-registered artillery would add to the onslaught. In this way, the commander would have committed the enemy to battle well beyond the safety of their own lines and 'locked' them into (*eingeschlossen*) a murderous open space. They would now be subjected to the *Eingreifen*: counter-attack by large numbers of rehearsed reserves, spearheaded by the newly formed *Sturmbataillone* of highly trained shock troops. The depth and elasticity of the physical defence allowed for reserves to be based well to the rear, uncommitted and beyond interdiction by even the heaviest artillery.

Making best use of limited manpower, it was an efficient, intelligent approach that gave the enemy nothing too tangible to focus their efforts against. Equally, the concentric repetitions of this system harnessed the expanse of French countryside at Germany's disposal.

The drawback for the defenders of Vimy Ridge was that, as described, the topography was not at all compatible with the theoretical application of the revised doctrine. The ridge drops off on its steepest, eastern side, between 1 and 4km behind the German front line. This makes any kind of defence in depth problematic. Von Fasbender was well aware that any resistance beyond the ridge would have to be far enough away so as not to be directly overlooked by a captured crest. The eastern gradient also created serious difficulties for counter-attack contingencies.

He had no choice but to retain the more conventional, 1916 approach to the physical defence of the ridge, relying on deep dugouts, concrete redoubts, and nests of fighting positions at key points. The trench lines were largely predictable, as were his forward-loaded dispositions as described in the previous chapter.

This is not to say that his defences were ineffective. Vicious wire entanglements and cunningly sited machine guns were much in evidence. In many parts, particularly south-east of Thelus, the *Zwischenstellung* was dug on a textbook gentle reverse slope with broad fields of fire.

In view of this, von Falkenhausen was not concerned. He felt that the imposing ground on the ridge precluded the necessity for complex defence in depth and placed his *Eingreifen* divisions in the vicinity of Douai, well to the rear as per official doctrine. A Canadian Corps intelligence summary made the following deduction:

> *Allowing two hours for entraining at Douai, travelling and detraining at Mericourt and 1¼ hours for the march, the first troops of the resting divisions could reach the Corps* [III Stellung] *line in 3¼ hours from the time of alarm. This calculation provides for trains being ready with steam up at Douai. It is assumed that trains will be ordered as soon as our final bombardment begins.*[4]

The *III Stellung* was still 5km east of Vimy. Von Fasbender's regimental reserve of resting battalions were assessed to be two hours from the *II Stellung* in the Lens–Vimy–Farbus vicinity but alone they were not sufficient to mount a significant counter-attack, especially to recapture a feature as imposing as Vimy Ridge.

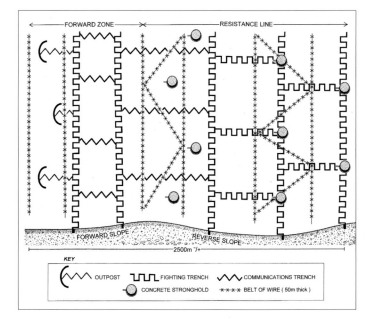

**This schematic illustrates the theory behind 'elastic defence'. In application, factors such as topography forced commanders to compromise in some areas.**

**Vimy Ridge from above the Douai Plain. The memorial marks the high point known as Hill 145. The *Zwischenstellung* and *II Stellung* are marked in red. *III Stellung* 'Corps Reserve' line was a further 5km east of the Ridge. (By permission of Tom Earl)**

In the German defence of Vimy Ridge, there was a dangerous misapplication of doctrine. Von Fasbender was correct in deducing that his ground was not suitable for 'elastic defence' but von Falkenhausen's counter-attacking divisions were not based accordingly. Probably under the influence of his dogmatic Chief of Staff, Oberst von Nagel, he applied the *Eingreifen* doctrine and placed them too far away.

In fairness, the precedent set by French attempts against Vimy Ridge left him supremely confident that any operation to capture it would take days to achieve, affording him ample time to fashion a counter-attack.

## CANADIAN CORPS' PLAN OF ATTACK

Broadly, the offensive failures of 1915 and 1916 can be explained by a series of frustrating paradoxes. As broached in the earlier examination of command, the challenge faced by allied commanders was how to protect infantry in the assault. In attempting to do so, certain patterns formed which seemed to offer no solution. The most significant perplexity was the interrelation between bombardment, consolidation and exploitation.

A protracted bombardment sought to destroy enemy fieldworks and to clear paths through wire sufficient to enable assault. Irrespective of the associated problems of effectiveness, it was always the perfect warning to German commanders that an attack was imminent, allowing them to prepare reserves. They held the advantage of interior lines – meaning that they had the use of road and rail to convey reinforcements faster than attacking formations could mass in numbers through the narrow gap in defences.

Short sharp bombardments were the surest way to achieve surprise but they would leave hapless battalions hung up in undamaged wire and at the mercy of strongpoints. To overcome this, the best chance that an attacker had was to rush lightly equipped troops across no man's land supported by

This photograph of a Canadian Corps ammunition dump illustrates the scale of the logistic effort required to mount the attack on Vimy Ridge. The number of animals tethered in the background is equally illuminating. (IWM, CO 2542)

**Plank road being constructed on Vimy Ridge. In preparation for the attack, Canadian Corps Labour Companies built 10km of plank road. (IWM, CO 1261)**

accurate mortar fire and smoke in abundance. This was always the chosen method for trench raids. However, in major attacks, where gains were to be held or exploited, troops had none of the equipment required to consolidate the position and insufficient ammunition to fight a protracted battle. If troops attacked carrying every necessary item of equipment, it was axiomatic that they tended not to make it across no man's land in the first place. This drew the emphasis back to the deliberate approach with all its associated problems.

In any event, exploitation of success was impossible at the operational level because the defending Germans still held the advantage of interior lines. They knew how decisive this advantage was and developed an entire doctrine based on it.

## DISTRIBUTION OF ARTILLERY AT VIMY RIDGE

| Division | Approx Frontage | Generic FA Bdes | Attached FA Bdes | 2in. Trench Mortars | 9.45in. Trench Mortars | Div. Heavy Art. Group | 9.2in. Howitzer Batteries | 8in. Howitzer Batteries | 6in. Howitzer Batteries | 60-pdr. Gun Batteries | 6in. Mark VII Gun Batteries | Remarks |
|---|---|---|---|---|---|---|---|---|---|---|---|---|
| 1st | 2,000m | 2 (8) | 4 (16) | 18 | 5 | 11th | 1 | 1 | 3 | Nil | Nil | No of Field Artillery Batteries is in brackets |
|  |  |  |  |  |  | 77th | 1 | 2 | 2 | Nil | Nil |  |
| 2nd | 1,400m | 2 (8) | 5 (20) | 18 | 5 | 64th | 1 | 2 | 2 | Nil | Nil | No of Field Artillery Batteries is in brackets |
|  |  |  |  |  |  | 70th | Nil | Nil | 4 | Nil | Nil |  |
| 3rd | 1,300m | 2 (8) | 2 (8) | 36 | 6 | 13th | 1 | 1 | 3 | Nil | Nil | No of Field Artillery Batteries is in brackets |
|  |  |  |  |  |  | 53rd | 1 | Nil | 3 | Nil | Nil |  |
| 4th | 2,000m | 2 (8) | 5 (20) | 24 | 4 | 1st (Can) | 1 | Nil | 4 | Nil | Nil | No of Field Artillery Batteries is in brackets |
|  |  |  |  |  |  | 51st | Nil | 2 | 3 | Nil | Nil |  |
| C/Bty Group 1 |  |  |  |  |  |  | 2 | 1 | 1 | 2 | – | Also 1x4.5in. Howitzer Bty |
| C/Bty Group 2 |  |  |  |  |  |  | Nil | Nil | Nil | 4 | 1 | Also 1x4.5in. Howitzer Bty |
| C/Bty Group 3 |  |  |  |  |  |  | Nil | 1 | 1 | 3 | – | Also 1x4.5in. Howitzer Bty |
| Total Batteries | 18-pdr. | 24 | 48 | 9 | 4 | N/A | 8 | 10 | 26 | 9 | 2 |  |
|  | 4.5in. | 8 | 16 |  |  |  |  |  |  |  |  |  |
| Total Guns | 18-pdr. | 160 | 320 | 96 | 24 |  | 36 | 36 | 104 | 54 | 8 | See Notes for explanation of odd totals |
|  | 4.5in. | 46 | 92 |  |  |  |  |  |  |  |  |  |

**Notes:**

**1.** All Field Artillery Batteries had six pieces, as did 60-pdr. Batteries. 6in. Mark VII Gun, 6, 8 and 9.2in. Howitzer Batteries all had four apiece. 2in. Trench Mortar Batteries had eight barrels; 9.45in. batteries had four.

**2.** In some instances, the 'Total Guns' figures do not conform to the set number of guns per battery. This is because some batteries were over established strength whilst others were suffering shortages. An obvious example of this is the 9.45in. Trench Mortar. Each battery was established for four mortars but three of four divisions were fielding extra.

A British orderly officer inspects fresh rations before they are carried up to the front line in Arras. Each brigade in the Canadian Corps had a dedicated ration-carrying company. The containers were insulated by hot water and always somehow tainted by food that had been in them before. To this day, British soldiers will attest to curry-flavoured tea. (IWM, Q4836)

Byng was warned about his likely task in December 1916 and he was abreast of the costly lessons learnt that year. Artillery was starting to be appreciated for its *application* rather than simply concentration of fire, and the imperative for protection during shock action had sown the seeds for innovations such as the tank, extended mining operations and sophisticated small unit tactics. Most telling of all was the acceptance that plans had to be based on limited objectives with 'breakthrough' as a contingency rather than the focus.

On the conceptual level, that realization was the decisive ingredient of success at Vimy Ridge. It set the parameters for meticulous and imaginative preparations.

Byng turned first to his Chief of Staff, the tall, dapper Brigadier-General Percy Pellexfen de Blaquire Radcliffe. A highly intelligent artilleryman, in the political arena of the General Staff he was a cunning ambassador for the Canadian Corps. The next man Byng and Radcliffe would have spoken to was arguably the most important of all – Brigadier-General George Farmer, Chief Administration Officer and logistician.

The scale of the logistic operation to support Byng's attack is staggering. Dominated then, as today, by the insatiable appetite of artillery, the corps was supplied by eight trains a day, each carrying 370 tonnes of stores. The breakdown was as follows: four for ammunition, one for engineering stores, one for road building and tramway stores, one for general supplies and one split between animal fodder and spare capacity at Farmer's discretion.

Those stores were unloaded into dumps and moved on by road or light rail tramway. All artillery ammunition was conveyed from the two railheads by tramway, 20km of which was laid as part of the build-up. Existing roads were woefully inadequate for the task and had to be improved or repaired by hard core. 10km of plank road was constructed to expand the network. Laid end to end, Farmer took delivery of 50km of timbers per day.

Motor transport was still the exception and the corps utilized 50,000 horses and mules. Each division managed a pack train of 180 animals with a further 225 per brigade and 55 for each battalion. Even so, the majority supported the artillery. Vets dealt with 1,000 casualties a day, mainly from accidents and sickness. It is ironic that most of the motor transport was used to move fodder.

The corps and its animals had a daily requirement of 600,000 gallons of water, supplied by six purpose-built reservoirs, 24 pumping installations and 72km of pipeline. Near the front line, a 227,500-litre reservoir was constructed 12m underground.

As a sample of requirements for the actual attack, Farmer indented for 24 million rounds of small arms ammunition, 450,000 grenades and 1,005,000 rounds of 18-pdr. gun ammunition. But the true measure of the challenge is to be found in the detail. His staff had to account for everything from tents, clothing and latrines to potatoes, razor blades, soap, and pencils.

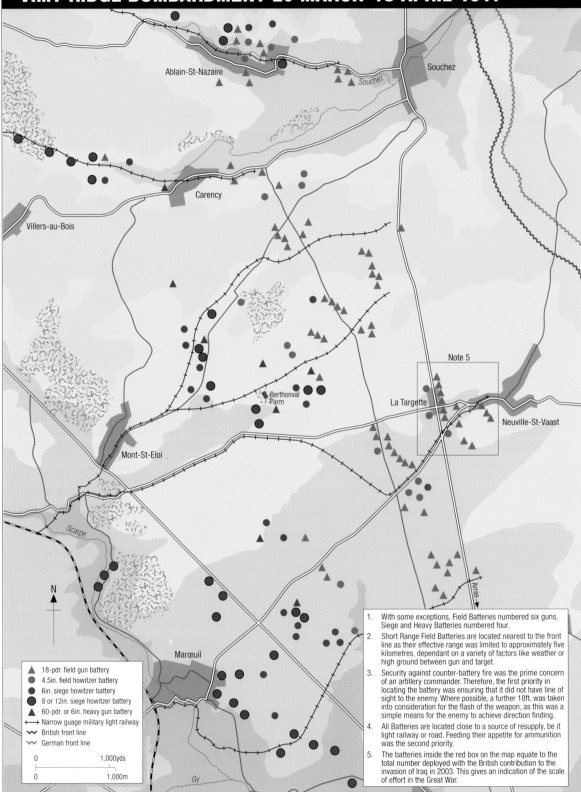

Ablain-St-Nazaire

Souchez

Souchez

Carency

Villers-au-Bois

Berthonval Farm

Note 5

La Targette

Neuville-St-Vaast

Mont-St-Eloi

Scarpe

Arras

N

Marœuil

Gy

**Legend**

▲ 18-pdr. field gun battery
● 4.5in. field howitzer battery
● 6in. siege howitzer battery
● 8 or 12in. siege howitzer battery
▲ 60-pdr. or 6in. heavy gun battery
—|—|— Narrow guage military light railway
〜 British front line
〜 German front line

0 — 1,000yds
0 — 1,000m

1. With some exceptions, Field Batteries numbered six guns, Siege and Heavy Batteries numbered four.

2. Short Range Field Batteries are located nearest to the front line as their effective range was limited to approximately five kilometres, dependant on a variety of factors like weather or high ground between gun and target.

3. Security against counter-battery fire was the prime concern of an artillery commander. Therefore, the first priority in locating the battery was ensuring that it did not have line of sight to the enemy. Where possible, a further 18ft. was taken into consideration for the flash of the weapon, as this was a simple means for the enemy to achieve direction finding.

4. All Batteries are located close to a source of resupply, be it light railway or road. Feeding their appetite for ammunition was the second priority.

5. The batteries inside the red box on the map equate to the total number deployed with the British contribution to the invasion of Iraq in 2003. This gives an indication of the scale of effort in the Great War.

Troops of the Canadian 4th Division lifting cases of Mills Bomb grenades using the traditional Native American Indian 'tumpline' method. Though it looks uncomfortable, veterans have attested to its effectiveness. Behind the centre figure can be seen a tempting supply of rum jars. (IWM, CO 1989)

The manpower bill was also significant. Everything that went forward to the line itself had to be man-packed. The Canadians were old hands at this and adopted timeless Native American techniques such as the tumpline. Predictably for the private soldier, this practice of bearing the load with a leather strap across the forehead made the burden no less onerous. Commanders simply doubled the amount a man was made to carry.

Each Canadian brigade had a dedicated tumpline company of 80 men. There was also a company for ferrying 'hot' rations (parentheses in honour of the thousands of men who probably ate cold stew each night). Labour companies also served the railheads, stores dumps, ammunition depots and road building parties. History seldom acknowledges these unglamorous characters. They shared many of the same dangers, toiled incessantly in foul weather and invariably received the sharp end of someone's tongue for mishaps lamentably beyond their control. Next time you see fearsome looking artillery shells in a museum, spare a thought for the men who had to lift them off the rail car every day.

Whilst arranging his resources, Byng was also busy gathering intelligence. With the enemy lines impermeable to infiltration it was a limited process. In addition to the summaries disseminated by GHQ and First Army (including information gleaned from informants in occupied France), he relied on aerial reconnaissance and interrogation of prisoners captured in trench raids.

The key piece of information sought from captured Germans was the regiment they were from. This was often betrayed by their uniform but normally they proved quite talkative and gave more away. Deserters, though not commonplace, were particularly forthcoming. This assessment of enemy dispositions was then married to the innumerable photographs and reports compiled by the Royal Flying Corps' daring reconnaissance pilots in their fragile Be2 aircraft. By April 1917, the intelligence picture was extremely accurate.

Byng also sanctioned information gathering of another sort. Major-General Arthur Currie, commanding the Canadian 1st Division, was sent to join a party of British GHQ staff officers to visit French units that had fought at Verdun. They hoped to draw on some of the many lessons identified there, particularly in relation to the co-operation of artillery with infantry. It was a worthwhile exercise but not as fruitful as they had expected because opinions varied so much.

Reaching the ridge with his infantry unscathed remained Byng's fixation. This started with their security in the approach. He did not want enemy artillery to interfere with his preliminary assembly, follow-on forces or re-supply. Communications trenches were too narrow, winding and confusing to rely on alone. The solution was to dig 12 tunnel systems – known as subways – beneath the forward trenches to assist the forward flow of men and *matériel* in complete security. Varying in length from 250m to nearly 2km, the subways contained forward headquarters, communications nodes, forward supply dumps, assembly areas for infantry companies and advanced dressing stations. At between 5 and 15m below ground, they were as invulnerable to shellfire as the dugouts inhabited by the Germans on the ridge.

British tunnelling companies constructed the subways as the Canadian miners were already employed on the Ypres sector. These men, coal miners or London Underground engineers in peacetime, worked 18-hour shifts, digging out the chalk by hand. In that context, the rate at which they mined was remarkable. One company managed nearly fifteen metres a day. The galleries were 2.25m high and approximately 1.25m wide but the miners also had to build large chambers for headquarters and other infrastructure. The subways terminated in the front line, sometimes into no man's land itself. In the latter instance, exits would be blown as the attack went in.

Explosive mining operations had been a feature of the war since the French started in 1915. The concept was medieval and the operating environment troglodyte. Saps were driven under the opposing side's lines, explosives packed into a chamber and then detonated as part of a raid or attack. The consequence was a no man's land pockmarked with enormous craters. The lips of craters were held as outposts, with opposing sentries sometimes no further apart than the length of a tennis court. The British inhabitants of the ridge had duelled with German miners throughout their tenure and now, to create shock effect, Byng planned to blow 18 mines under the German front line as the attack went in.

Subtle as all this subterranean activity was, Byng's foremost means of protecting his infantry was the artillery at his disposal. This fact was not lost on General Sir Henry Horne either and he put the weight of First Army's artillery effort behind the Canadians. He gave Byng all three of his heavy artillery groups, four extra divisional artillery groups and (less obvious but most significant of all) the overwhelming share of his ammunition allocation. There was an artillery piece to every 10m of corps frontage – a greater concentration than seen at the Somme the previous year (see table on page 32).

Since then the BEF had learnt not to place their faith in simple weight of fire. Byng sat down with his chief gunner, Brigadier-General 'Dinky' Morrison, looked at the type and number of weapons at their disposal and prioritized all conceivable tasks for the artillery. Fire planning had to factor in the comparative range of weapons, their accuracy, rate of fire, type of ammunition and relative mobility. This might seem obvious now but in 1914, field guns still fired over open sights at targets they could see. Co-ordination of massed indirect artillery fire was comparatively novel.

Byng knew that he was going to have to soften up the German defences considerably if his infantry were to survive but not at the expense of all semblance of surprise. He compromised on a 20-day bombardment, thorough but unpredictable. By virtue of its duration and distinct variations in intensity, the Germans would be confused and worn down. It mattered not that there was ample warning. His objectives were limited. After three weeks of false alarms and no marked increase in severity immediately before the assault, *relative* surprise could still be achieved.

For the preparatory phases of the bombardment, Byng set four priorities: counter-battery fire, destruction of fighting positions, destruction of wire, and interdiction of re-supply and repair parties.

**The Grange Subway as it is today. Omit the plastic lights; replace concrete with timber and it is completely unchanged. The glass insulators just visible above the left-hand light fixtures were for telegraph and field telephone communication cable. Chalk could conduct the traffic to enemy listening devices. (Author's collection)**

OPPOSITE **This appendix to *Instructions For The Training Of Platoons For Offensive Action, 1917* sets out the basic doctrine for a platoon attack against its objective. Clearly, this is only a textbook representation but the theory is evident and it was applied to great effect on Vimy Ridge. (Reproduced by kind permission of the Imperial War Museum)**

# APPENDIX VIII.

# TRENCH TO TRENCH ATTACK
## PLATOON IN 1st WAVE
## MEETING A POINT OF RESISTANCE.

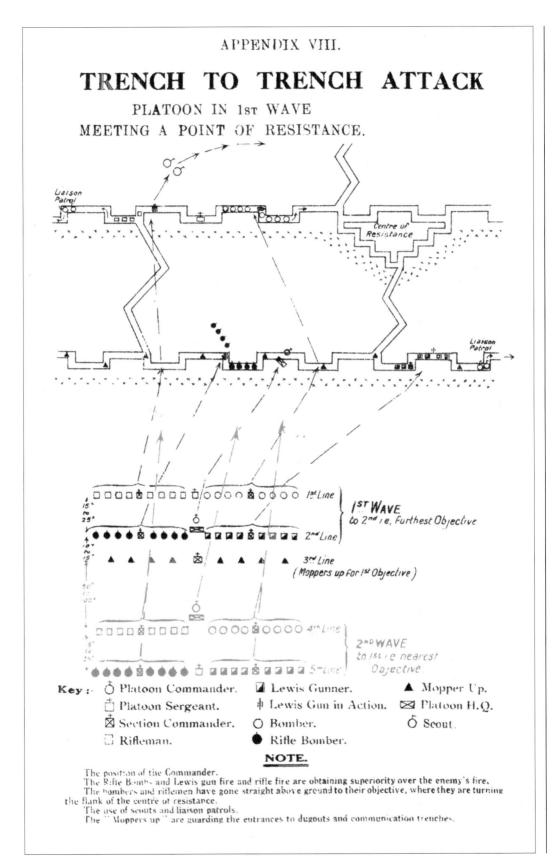

**Key :—**

| | | |
|---|---|---|
| Ȯ Platoon Commander. | Lewis Gunner. | ▲ Mopper Up. |
| Platoon Sergeant. | Lewis Gun in Action. | ⊠ Platoon H.Q. |
| ⊠ Section Commander. | ○ Bomber. | Ȯ Scout. |
| Rifleman. | ● Rifle Bomber. | |

## NOTE.

The position of the Commander.

The Rifle Bombs and Lewis gun fire and rifle fire are obtaining superiority over the enemy's fire.

The bombers and riflemen have gone straight above ground to their objective, where they are turning the flank of the centre of resistance.

The use of scouts and liaison patrols.

The "Moppers up" are guarding the entrances to dugouts and communication trenches.

A Canadian infantry company receives a brief from an officer. This scene was repeated on a daily basis during the preparations for the assault. Troops became almost exasperated by the repetition of drills and rehearsals but later would admit their value. (IWM, CO 957)

To place counter-battery fire at the top of his priorities was one of Byng's most significant displays of prescience. It was understood that enemy artillery posed a grave threat to attacking infantry but the difficulty had always been locating it. In light of this, Byng appointed Lieutenant-Colonel Andrew McNaughton as his counter-battery officer. McNaughton was a pioneering Canadian gunner with imagination and a grasp of the science behind direction finding. He recruited other enthusiastic exponents of this fledgling discipline and created a specialist staff. They were to make a telling contribution.

Going into the attack itself, Byng planned to protect his infantry with a complex, split-second 'creeping barrage'. Contrary to some claims, this was not an innovation born at Vimy Ridge. The concept was first attempted at Loos two years previously. Nonetheless, by 1917 it had accrued a great deal of sophistication. This linear barrage of light field guns would precede the attacking infantry by as little as 75m, lifting at set intervals of three minutes or more. If all went according to plan, the barrage would keep German forces in their dugouts until the Canadians were on top of them.

Horne also gave the Canadians eight Mark II tanks in support but Byng did not feel that they were entirely suitable for his task. In their infancy, tanks were slow and unreliable and the ridge was a morass of flooded shell holes just waiting to bog them down.

Byng did not put all his faith in this fire support to his battalions. He also directed an exhaustive examination of low-level infantry tactics and training. In February 1917, the British General Staff issued a short pamphlet entitled *Instructions for the training of platoons for offensive action*. It heralded a return to the pre-war emphasis on 'fire and movement'[5] and added the contribution of a dedicated section of 'bombers' (hand grenade men) as well as the use of 'rifle-bombers'[6] and the Lewis light machine-gun section for suppression of enemy strongpoints. These tactics will be explained in more detail later but in planning terms, the key lay in training.

The German World War II Field Marshal Erwin Rommel, who was a young infantry officer at the Battle of Caporetto in 1917, once said, 'the best form of welfare is training'. Byng was equally passionate about his responsibility for preparing troops thoroughly for the task ahead. As Rommel alluded, it is the surest way to keep them alive.

GOC Artillery, Canadian Corps – Brigadier-General Edward Morrison. Byng referred to him by his nickname, 'Dinky'. His was a massive responsibility at Vimy Ridge. He deserves much of the credit for the success. (IWM, CO 2224)

A Canadian infantryman coming out of the line in early March 1917. (IWM, CO 1027)

Major-General Arthur Currie, GOC, 1st Canadian Division. A big but unassuming man, Currie was highly talented and followed Byng into command of the Canadian Corps for the last year of the war. It was no less than he deserved. He was cautious yet innovative, a difficult balance to strike. (IWM, CO 1540)

In training his men, Byng developed the tactical doctrine for small units by issuing platoons with specific objectives. This gave them focus and allowed them to rehearse. Full-scale drills were conducted in the rear areas with tape representing trenches and officers with flags displaying the progress of the creeping barrage. Currie was even more vehement about this process and drilled his division to the point of tedium. Every single man in the attack was made to file past scale models of their objectives. Byng encouraged every officer and senior non-commissioned officer to visit the vast plasticine model of Vimy Ridge near First Army headquarters. Nobody was under any illusions that the affair would be bloodless. Every soldier was made to learn the job of the man alongside him and more importantly, above him. 45,000 maps were issued so that platoon sergeants and section commanders had them as well.[7]

In the confusion that would abound on the ridge, Byng wanted to ensure that his men could communicate – particularly with the guns. His signallers laid over 1,440km of cable for telegraph and field telephone. All cabling within five miles of the front was buried to a regulation depth of seven feet in separated bundles of 35 pairs. To achieve this, labourers dug over 34km of trench by hand. Follow-on forces were directed to unreel massive coils of cable as they advanced forward. Byng knew how frail this connection would be so he also resourced attacking formations with Very pistol flares and bright panels to lay on the ground. He then planned for 'contact patrols' to be flown by reconnaissance aircraft over the battlefield at regular intervals. They would spot the panels and radio back reports on the limit of advance. This was crucial if the barrage plans were to retain any flexibility whatsoever.

In accordance with the overall plan for the Arras front, Vimy Ridge was sub-divided into coloured objective lines – Black, Red, Blue and Brown (se map on page 51). The barrage would 'pause' at these objectives while fresh troops prepared to resume the advance. The broad southern sector was given to Currie's 1st Division. Above him was Burstall's 2nd Division with the devastated village of Thelus to contend with. Lipsett's 3rd Division was tasked with the narrower central area of the ridge, including La Folie Farm. The highest point of the ridge, Hill 145, was given to Watson's 4th Division. As a follow-on operation he would also have to capture the spur above the village of Givenchy-en-Gohelle to the north of Vimy Ridge. This heavily defended knoll was nicknamed 'The Pimple'. To assist the follow-on operation, the British 73rd Brigade from I Corps' 24th Division would storm Bois-en-Hache to the north of the Souchez River.

Byng kept a healthy reserve – 15th and 95th Brigades from 5th Division and 9th Brigade from his 3rd Division. They were given three contingencies to prepare for: the relief of troops in forward positions to assist consolidation, the capture of 'The Pimple' if 4th Division was exhausted and exploitation operations.

Byng was not naive about the chances of his plans being disrupted but he appreciated the true benefit of such extensive preparation. His men were confident.

4 The National Archive (TNA), Public Records Office (PRO), WO/95/3838.
5 Defined by a portion of the force laying down accurate suppressive fire while the remainder dash forward.
6 A grenade fired by a blank cartridge from a cup attachment on the end of the rifle. They had a range of up to 100 yards though accuracy was entirely dependent on the skill of the firer.
7 Wide issue of mapping is a measure often attributed to Byng alone but in fact, it had been in practice since the Somme in 1916.

# THE CAPTURE OF VIMY RIDGE

## PRELIMINARY OPERATIONS

I n co-ordination with Nivelle's plans, 9 April – Easter Monday – was the date set for the Arras offensive. To the planners it was known as 'Z-Day'. In reality, the capture of Vimy Ridge started well in advance of that date. Extensive preliminary operations were a vital part of the effort and warrant considerable attention, especially since they cost both sides many lives.

### Raiding

Raiding was both a routine activity and, as has been described, a crucial method of intelligence gathering. Exercised across the Western Front, raids varied in scale from a handful of cut-throats scrambling over no man's land in the dark to entire battalions executing set-piece attacks with artillery and machine-gun support. The binding definition of a raid was that any stay in the enemy line was temporary. Gains were not consolidated.

British military doctrine encouraged raiding in the interests of 'offensive spirit', almost as if the intelligence benefit was a by-product rather than the desired end. Undoubtedly many raids were unnecessary and wasteful – particularly the calamitous efforts used to 'blood' new troops. The Kirke Report of 1931 (*Lessons learnt in the Great War*) admits to 'an excessively aggressive raiding policy'.

When the Canadians arrived on Vimy Ridge they wanted to make their mark. Christmas of 1916 witnessed many raids, giving rise to a

The winter of 1916/17 was especially bitter. Despite all the raiding activity and preparations for a spring offensive, the tedium and privation of trench routine was the enduring experience for most. (IWM, Q10620)

sense of competition among different battalions. Princess Patricia's Canadian Light Infantry developed a reputation for tenacity and daring, as did the 22nd Battalion of French Canadians – the 'Van Doos'.[8] Raiding became increasingly spectacular as the divisions tried to outdo each other. It reached a climax in January 1917 when the 20th and 21st Battalions mounted a joint effort involving over 800 men. In examples of this magnitude, raiders would remain in the captured trenches for hours, laying waste to everything. Dugouts and ammunition dumps were blasted with satchel charges, rations spoiled, water tainted or poured away, and enemy troops killed or captured.

Captured prisoners were not the only aspect of intelligence value. The condition of trenches and protective wire was a reflection of the discipline of its occupants and the effectiveness of any bombardment. Aerial photographs were limited in what they could portray. For example, only men on the ground could confirm the abandonment of fighting positions and the reporting of an absence of enemy was often as useful as finding them. In the reconnaissance world, this is known as 'negative information'.

Smaller raids were essentially fighting patrols. Normally led by a young officer, they were mostly volunteers. In any large body of soldiers, there are always those characters with the ruthless zeal for that kind of duty. Trench raiders looked more like pirates than soldiers, arming themselves with all manner of improvised weapons. Punch daggers, nailed maces, knuckle-dusters, spring coshes, garrottes and hatchets were all prevalent. In his memoir *Goodbye to All That*, Robert Graves even reports seeing men armed with home-made pikes. Grenades and firearms were not the first resort at this level because the noise would just stir up a hornet's nest of flares, fixed-arc machine guns and mortar fire. In the early hours of a moonless night, German sentries must have dreaded a raid. The prospect of a sudden violent rush by ten thugs with blackened faces would test any man's courage.

Larger raids were more complex affairs and would need to be preceded by reconnaissance patrols. Sometimes involving just two men, these patrols demanded considerable nerve. Armed with just a revolver and one or two grenades, the men would crawl forward having tied bootlaces about themselves to avoid snagging clothing on wire. A Canadian 3rd Division intelligence summary dated 5 April 1917, describes one such operation:

> *A patrol from 1st CMR under Lt. Wier and Acting Corporal Tait made a daylight reconnaissance between 6 and 7pm of no man's land and the enemy post on B4 crater. This post was found to be unoccupied. Three men were seen in FLY trench grid A.4.a.78.74. On seeing the patrol they ran towards FLAPPER. Cpl. Tait emptied his revolver at them, hitting one man and Lt. Wier used one clip of his revolver on a man who exposed himself on the eastern lip of B4 crater.*[9]

Having established that a section of enemy frontline trench was vulnerable, the raid would be planned carefully and rehearsed on tape mock-ups in the rear areas. Patrols cut lanes through both friendly and enemy wire, leaving it in place to be pulled aside as the raid went in.

In terms of execution, the first requirement was to isolate that portion of the line. By 1917, the BEF had perfected the 'box barrage', which prevented counter-attack by sealing the area with continuous indirect fire until the raid was over. Field guns played their part but the favoured weapon for this kind of work was the Stokes 3in. trench mortar because of its high rate of fire and accuracy.

Machine guns provided suppressive fire, sweeping the enemy parapet as the raiders rushed forward. Parties were organized specific to task. Lewis gun teams were pushed ahead to cover the withdrawal and provide suppression of depth positions as necessary. A reserve sheltered in no man's land ready to assist with the extraction of casualties and prisoners whilst the raiding detail split into six to twelve-man teams, bombing their way up the trenches in all directions.

Success lay in split-second timing, aggression and a fast withdrawal once the operation was concluded. Enemy response would be equally hostile, with pre-registered artillery fires seeking to cut off the raiders from escape.

After-action reports are always dry. A 43rd Battalion raid under the command of Lt. Fowler reads:

*Found crater post unoccupied. Two sentries at the junction of the frontline and the sap were captured. Two of the enemy were killed in the trenches; two dugouts alleged to contain 26 men were bombed.*[10]

Language so businesslike conceals the reality. Heads opened up by the cleaving of vicious improvised weapons, sentries shot in the back as they tried to scuttle away down communications trenches and men blasted or entombed in their dugouts by ammonal charges. Raiders also suffered: the frantic withdrawal encumbered by a wounded comrade, tired legs getting snagged in wire just long enough to draw the attention of a distant marksman. It was an ugly aspect to an already baneful existence.

Major General Currie ordered the very last raid before the offensive opened. On Sunday 8 April, a reconnaissance aircraft reported that the enemy wire to his front was still heavy. Ground observers reported it gone. The subsequent raid by 2nd Brigade's 10th Battalion confirmed that it was still an effective obstacle, triggering a renewed bombardment to finish the job.

**The battle for air superiority**
Reconnaissance was the primary role for aircraft in 1917. This fundamental responsibility was split between straightforward observation, specialist aerial photography and artillery forward air control. With all these tasks being best achieved by having unlimited use of enemy airspace, there was a burgeoning requirement for dedicated fighter formations. The resulting struggle for air superiority became a violent and costly affair.

The Royal Flying Corps (RFC) was the fastest expanding corps in the BEF. In the period from July 1916 to April 1917, the number of squadrons on the Western Front grew from 28 to 50. Opposite the British front, the Germans could only operate 264 aircraft, a third of Britain's 754 total. Consequently, the RFC adopted a highly aggressive posture, forcing the Germans to focus their efforts on the defence of their own airspace. This protected British preparations from detailed observation by German planes. The Germans exacted a high price for this status quo.

A BE2c aircraft as used by 16 Squadron, Royal Flying Corps. Its 90hp engine gave it an air speed of up to 80mph. It was armed with machine guns but was primarily designed as a reconnaissance aircraft and, where possible, flew with fighter protection. (IWM, Q15590)

Baron Manfred von Richthofen climbing into his Albatross CIX fighter. The DIII model Albatross was more prevalent at the battle of Arras but both were almost identical in performance. Audacity and aggresion compensated for German inferiority in numbers. (IWM, Q 67137)

Their Albatross DIII outperformed all models of British aircraft.[11] In the first week of April alone, the RFC lost 131 aircraft – 76 to enemy action and 56 to accidents. It was to become known as 'Bloody April'.

At Vimy, the Canadian Corps had 16 Squadron RFC on permanent attachment. Equipped with the slow and largely obsolete BE2c, they were protected by I Corps' 2 Squadron with its FE2b 'pusher' planes (so-called because the propeller was mounted at the back). First Army also gave Byng the use of 8 (Naval), 25, 40 and 43 Squadrons from its 10th (Army) Wing. These were used for a variety of roles including deep offensive patrolling and balloon attack.

16 Squadron was employed exclusively for observation and artillery co-operation. Under their charismatic commander, Major P. C. Maltby, these daring pilots made a decisive contribution. They were indispensable to the intelligence effort and worked particularly hard to support Lt. Col. McNaughton's counter-battery cell.

Their daily forays over the ridge and ground beyond were perilous in the extreme. These aircraft could only manage speeds we would associate with a car and the flying patterns required for observation and

A camera fitted to a BE2c aircraft. Do not be misled by the improvised mount and primitive equipment. They produced imagery of superb fidelity. Altitude and orientation in flight were also carefully logged to assist survey. (IWM, Q33850)

photography were by their nature, predictable. The escorting FE2bs would fly above them, ready to pounce on any German fighters that arrived to interfere. When they did, chaos would ensue as the formations scattered into a confused mêlée.

The dogfights were a compelling spectacle for the men in trenches beneath and they followed the shifting fortunes like a soap opera. This tendency was abetted by the presence of Baron Manfred von Richthofen's 'Flying Circus' squadron with their distinctive red paint schemes. Von Richthofen alone accounted for 30 British aircraft during the Arras offensive. Contrary to popular notions of chivalry, the war was just as ruthless for airmen as it was for the infantry; crashed aircraft were routinely strafed and balloon observers were machine-gunned while descending from their stricken gondolas on parachutes.

The audacity of these pilots brought with it a degree of eccentricity. The captured co-pilot/observer of one German aircraft that crash-landed over Vimy Ridge was an inebriated officer wearing full mess dress with spurs. When questioned, the pilot explained that his squadron officers had held a dinner the previous night. It had not finished until daybreak and the character in question had stepped straight from the party into his plane for the morning's sortie.

### The symphony of hell

It is sometimes said that World War I was an artilleryman's war fought by the infantry. Certainly, never has artillery been so singularly dominant. First it colluded with the machine gun to drive the combatants below ground and then bred rapaciously to meet the demands of the siege war *it* created. Following its development through the period is almost like tracing the emergence of a dominant species. Artillery's pre-eminence was not challenged until the more dynamic battles of 1918 gave relevance to its relative immobility.

The bombardment in support of the Vimy Ridge attack was due to commence at 'Z minus 20' – 20 March – and was split into five phases. Phase One covered the period leading up to Z minus 20, when the guns

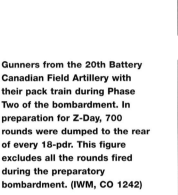

Unloading shells from a light rail tramway. This photograph was taken at Ypres but it is an accurate depiction of gun lines across the front in 1917. The delicate driving bands at the base of the shells have been bandaged to protect them from the elements. (IWM, Q5855)

Gunners from the 20th Battery Canadian Field Artillery with their pack train during Phase Two of the bombardment. In preparation for Z-Day, 700 rounds were dumped to the rear of every 18-pdr. This figure excludes all the rounds fired during the preparatory bombardment. (IWM, CO 1242)

convened on the area and supplies of ammunition were stockpiled. The first fortnight of the barrage formed Phase Two, with the final week being Phase Three. Phase Four was the direct support to the assault, and Phase Five outlined contingencies for consolidation and exploitation of any gains. The operation was underpinned by the priorities established in the previous chapter.

Aside from the massive logistic effort, Phase One was a question of establishing dispositions and command arrangements for the enormous array of artillery weapons at Byng's disposal (see map on page 34). All the extra field artillery brigades were distributed around the four divisions in the line. A division normally had just two field artillery brigades, each broken down into three batteries of 18-pdr. guns and one battery of 4.5in. howitzer, all at six pieces per battery.

Command of all field artillery was exercised at divisional level. Each division was also allocated two of the eight heavy artillery groups. As the

An 18-pdr. gun being realigned by its crew during the battle of Arras. It is not always acknowledged that the overwhelming majority of artillery pieces in World War I were light field guns like this one. The hulking howitzers and railway guns seen so often in documentary footage were a sparse asset. (IWM, Q5171)

table on page 32 shows, attachments were weighted to account for length of frontage, depth of objectives and density of enemy defences. Brigadier-General Massie (as GOC HA) supervised all heavy artillery fire plans. He also retained the four 12in. howitzers and three 15in. howitzers for specific corps level targeting.

Responsibility for counter-battery fires was assigned to three dedicated heavy artillery groups under the command of Massie. Each of these was augmented by one 4.5in. howitzer battery from the field artillery pool for the purposes of dealing with rapid counter-battery requests like *Minenwerfer* in the front line.

One hundred and fifty of the 358 Vickers machine guns in the Canadian Corps were apportioned to support the bombardment, including the 38 guns in Colonel Raymond Brutinel's Motor Machine-Gun Brigade. A passionate disciple of the machine gun and himself a wealthy entrepreneur, Brutinel created the brigade with the help of millionaire Canadian benefactors and ran it almost like a private army. He sold his ideas for indirect machine-gun fire to anyone who would listen. Clearly, Brigadier-General Morrison was a convert because indirect harassing fires were to play a major – and effective – part in the operation.

Locating the batteries was the next challenge thrown up by Phase One, logistics being the major consideration. A single 9.2in. howitzer required four supply lorries if it was not adjacent to a light railway. The guns also needed to be in ground 'dead' to the enemy so that they would be hidden from view. On firing, an 18-pdr. gave off a 4.5m flash. This necessitated at least 6m of cover between gun lines and the enemy. Finally, obvious as it sounds, the guns needed to be in a position to support planned advances on Z-Day. Even though the lightest models had moderate mobility, their ammunition trains did not.

Fortunately, the ground to the west of Vimy Ridge was kind to the problem and battery commanders were not often forced to compromise. Given that there were 987 mortars, guns, and howitzers to deploy, it was still no small achievement. Such a density of guns must

A 9.2in. howitzer on the Arras front, 1 April 1917. The recoil of this weapon was sufficient to topple it over so designers fitted a removable 'earth box' to the front end. A classic piece of civilian design intervention in the procurement process, this box took 12 hours of spadework to fill and had to be emptied again by hand when the gun moved. (IWM, Q6460)

have been an impressive sight; just as well that German aircraft were such a rarity.

Phase Two opened as planned on 20 March. In the interest of security, Byng decided to use only half of his available artillery for this phase. The decision had two associated benefits. It conserved ammunition, allowing for large stockpiles to be accumulated in anticipation of later phases, and it preserved barrel life. Barrel wear degrades accuracy and is suffered at a greater rate when longer-range shoots necessitate larger propellant charges. Being a highly professional gunner, Morrison appreciated this problem and reserved his barrel lives for the extended ranges that the planned objectives would demand.

The counter-battery effort during this phase was focused on locating the enemy guns. Colonel McNaughton's team was busy toiling with an array of curious-looking scientific equipment. They used two main methods: sound ranging and flash spotting. Sound ranging was achieved by recording the vibrations of passing shells with numerous oscillographs. The interrelation of these readings allowed the analysts to create a three-dimensional duplicate of the shell's trajectory. Flash spotting was accomplished by triangulating the sightings of observers in the RFC's 1st Kite Balloon Squadron. They would signal an enemy gun flash with a buzzer that relayed into McNaughton's headquarters, and then log the direction against a serial number. Later, the counter-battery team would cross-reference these sightings, using their own record of buzzer soundings to establish which serial numbers applied to which gun flash. It was painstaking but once perfected both systems were producing readings accurate to 10m.

Decisions on whether to act on those readings depended on confirmatory over-flights by 16 Squadron. Enemy batteries could be struck in advance but there was a danger that they would simply move and necessitate a repetition of the whole process. For this reason, most were left alone until the final stages. Of nearly 300 artillery pieces at *Gruppe Vimy's* disposal, only 15 had been destroyed or damaged by 5 April.

Shelling of other enemy positions on the ridge was systematic. Phase Two focused on the forward lines because it was easier to hamper their repair with nocturnal harassing fires than it was the rear areas. The destruction of wire was entrusted to the 18-pdr. batteries and trench mortars.

Problems associated with this task are well documented, particularly in relation to the Somme in 1916 where the majority of the artillery ammunition was shrapnel. These shells had negligible effect on thick entanglements. The answer appeared to lie in the application of high explosive but here Vimy Ridge posed another challenge. The soft, churned-up ground on the ridge absorbed high explosive shells so that even with point detonation fuses, the effect was minimal. The solution was found in the brand new Mark 106 super-quick fuse. Highly sensitive, this fuse would detonate its charge instantly at first graze. They were still in short supply but the target effect was astonishing. Mortars were also good wire cutters. Their more sedate ballistics mitigated the effects of soft ground on impact fuses.

The Germans retaliated with their own artillery and inflicted losses, but their guns were hopelessly outnumbered. Kronprinz Rupprecht's Army Group had 419 7.7cm field guns, whereas the First and Third

A superb photograph of German wire being destroyed by trench mortars. The most destructive model was the 9.45in. 'Flying Pig'. Aptly named, it launched a massive projectile with a beguilingly gentle visible flight path. It was advisable to use that time to run for cover because the resulting explosion was decidedly unforgiving. (IWM, CO 1452)

Armies opposing him were able to muster 1,404 of the comparable 18-pdrs. Moreover, von Fasbender had to be careful about unmasking his guns because the counter-battery effort was so concerted.

When Phase Three opened on Z minus 6, its intensity broke windows in Douai, 20km away.

Germans later referred to this seven-day onslaught as the 'Symphony of Hell' and 'Week of Suffering'. The Canadian Corps artillery operations order stipulated, 'total available disclosure'. Ammunition allocations illustrate the true scale. Active 9.2in. howitzers fired 350 rounds in the first two weeks, while the 18-pdrs. fired 460. In Phase Three they fired 600 and 1,050 respectively. The shelling was conducted around the clock, giving the hapless Germans no respite from the incarceration of their airless dugouts. During the one hour a day that firing ceased to allow 16 Squadron to conduct battle damage assessments, Brutinel's Vickers guns would send thousands of rounds arcing onto the junctions and entrances of communications trenches to deter reliefs, ration parties and repair details. The already-shattered villages of Thelus, Les Tilleuls, Farbus, Givenchy-en-Gohelle, Vimy, Petit Vimy and Willerval were levelled to rubble. Hitherto spared German concrete strongpoints were smashed by massive, moaning howitzer shells whose detonation knocked the wind out of men nearly a kilometre away from impact.

On the battery positions, the gunners were stripped to the waist in spite of the cold weather. Even the lighter pieces like the 18-pdr. required a six-man crew – three men on the gun itself, two ammunition orderlies and a commander. They toiled in the acrid propellant fumes, loading and firing the weapon, preparing the ammunition and re-aligning the trail. It was also dangerous work. Defective fuses were commonplace and could cause a shell to detonate as it left the barrel. For the Germans on the ridge though, it was horrendous.

Deprived of sleep, food and air, all they could do was sit it out. Their own batteries were destroyed or ineffective and as infantrymen they had to contend with the frustration of being unable to remedy their plight. Those forced above ground to convey messages or ferry supplies had to negotiate the blitz through a confusion of totally unrecognizable trenches. Feints wore nerves further. The bombardment intensified for a few hours followed by a creeping barrage. They would 'stand to' their positions only to discover a false alarm. By Z-Day, they would actually welcome attack.

Von Fasbender knew that it was imminent. Canadians captured when raiding German lines had indicated that the bombardment was the prelude to attack. He requested artillery reinforcements. On 5 April, von Ludendorff himself issued a hastening order but the batteries would not be available until the 10th at the earliest. Neither von Fasbender nor von Ludendorff was to blame. Von Falkenhausen was the prevailing influence. He had not committed reserve divisions and refused to move their field artillery units forward. Artillery arriving from other formations was struggling to draw ammunition and get into position.

This attitude was not a consequence of incompetence, just complacency. As explained earlier in the narrative, he genuinely felt that there was no cause for alarm. His assessment (shared by von Nagel) was that the reserves were better employed improving the *Wotan II* line – an army group reserve line in the mould of the Hindenburg Line – and training. His argument was that they would clog the already jammed routes that should be assisting the artillery effort. Eventually, he was overruled and on 6 April, 18th Bavarian Infantry Division and elements of 1st Guards Reserve Corps were moved up to Douai and held on a reduced notice to move.

In *Gruppe Souchez*, Wichura had ordered his 11th Infantry Regiment of 16th Bavarian Infantry Division to conduct a spoiling attack opposite 'The Pimple'. Assisted by gas discharge, they intended to push their front line west of the feature thereby decreasing its vulnerability to capture. Operation *Munich*, as it was code-named, had to be cancelled owing to unfavourable wind conditions and the effects of Byng's bombardment.

**First Army Mk VII 6in. converted naval gun firing at night. Although almost impossible to observe and adjust their fire at night, the nightly bombardments prevented repair of damaged defences and deprived the Germans of any respite. (IWM, CO 1323)**

German 'Black Line' objectives under bombardment. The Canadian front line is in the middle distance. The men visible in the foreground are moving down a communications trench. (IWM, CO 1196)

## Final preparations and assembly

Total Canadian casualties sustained during the period from 22 March to 5 April were 11 officers and 326 other ranks killed with 60 officers and 1,256 other ranks wounded and missing. Raiding activity and the effects of German artillery retaliation were the principal causes. Although this figure equates to approximately 10 per cent of the total for the Vimy Ridge operation, preliminary operations doubtless saved thousands of lives during the attack itself.

For the thousands of infantrymen in the rest areas to the west of the Mont St Eloi heights, all that remained was to break camp and march to the forward assembly areas. Since 3 March, manning of the front line had been re-configured to fit the plan of attack, I Corps' 24th Division assuming responsibility for the line opposite Souchez. It was still a massive undertaking to organize the final movements, especially since security necessitated arrival in the hours of darkness. Staff officers planned it carefully, issuing movement orders well in advance. The operation was staggered over three days and they reduced the bombardment to a minimum in order not to provoke retaliatory fire while the approaches were so congested with men.

Troops boxed up their non-essential belongings, had a hot meal and then mustered for an inspection of weapons and iron rations.[12] The commanding officer or company commander would take this opportunity to address the men before they tramped up the road to the battalion's supply dump to draw ammunition and stores. With the exception of the leading assault platoons, Byng insisted on full fighting equipment scales. Burdened infantry was a calculated risk, as he wanted to ensure that gains were properly consolidated.

Dumping their greatcoats in the assembly areas, the Canadians each carried 170 rounds of ammunition (120 in pouches and 50 in reserve), two Mills bombs (15 for bombers and 12 for rifle bombers),[13] bayonet, gasmask, 48-hours' iron rations, two water bottles, sandbags, rubber groundsheet, and two signal flares. The Lewis gun sections carried 30 drum magazines between them. Each Battalion was issued 130 shovels, 66 picks and 200 pairs of wire cutters to distribute. Company HQ also carried air marker panels.

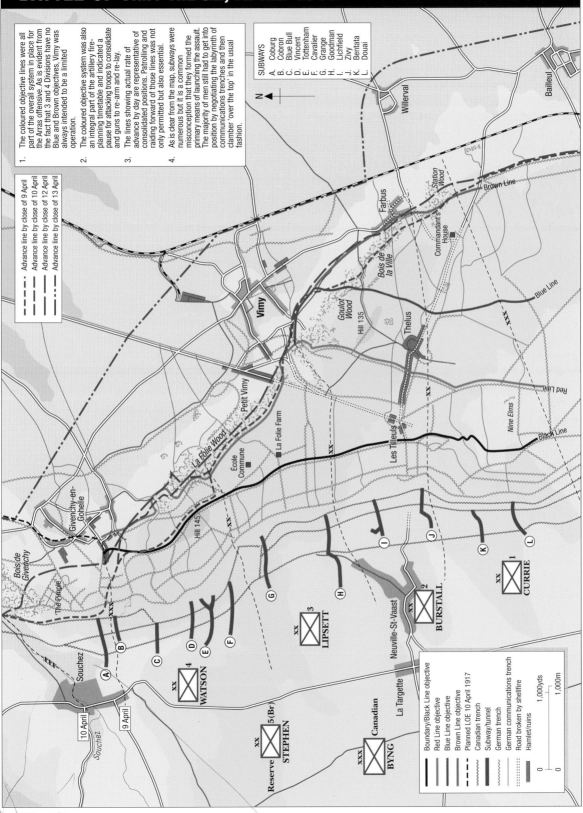

1. The coloured objective lines were all part of the overall system in place for the Arras offensive. As is evident from the fact that 3 and 4 Divisions have no Blue and Brown objectives, Vimy was always intended to be a limited operation.

2. The coloured objective system was also an integral part of the artillery fire-planning timetable and indicated a pause for attacking troops to consolidate and guns to re-arm and re-lay.

3. The lines showing actual rate of advance by day are representative of consolidated positions. Patrolling and raiding forward of those lines was not only permitted but also essential.

4. As is clear from the map, subways were numerous but it is a common misconception that they formed the primary means of launching the assault. The majority of men still had to get into position by negotiating the labyrinth of communications trenches and then clamber 'over the top' in the usual fashion.

**SUBWAYS**
A. Coburg
B. Cobron
C. Blue Bull
D. Vincent
E. Tottenham
F. Cavalier
G. Grange
H. Goodman
I. Lichfield
J. Zivy
K. Bentata
L. Douai

N ←

- – – – – Advance line by close of 9 April
- – – – – Advance line by close of 10 April
- – – – – Advance line by close of 12 April
- – – – – Advance line by close of 13 April

Balleul

Willerval

Station Wood

Brown Line

Farbus

Commandant's House

Bois de la Ville

Blue Line

Goulot Wood

Hill 135

Thelus

XXX

Vimy

XX

Red Line

Petit Vimy

Nine Elms

La Folie Wood

La Folie Farm

École Commune

Les Tilleuls

Black Line

XX

Givenchy-en-Gohelle

Bois de Giverchy

The Pimple

Hill 145

XXXX

Hill 145

XX

I

J

K

L

Souchez

A    B    C    D  E    F    G    H

XX
3
LIPSETT

XX
2
BURSTALL

XX
1
CURRIE

Neuville-St-Vaast

XX
4
WATSON

La Targette

10 April

9 April

Souchez

XX
5(Br)
STEPHEN

Reserve

XXX
Canadian
BYNG

**Legend**
- Boundary/Black Line objective
- Red Line objective
- Blue Line objective
- Brown Line objective
- Planned LOE 10 April 1917
- Canadian trench
- Subway/tunnel
- German trench
- German communications trench
- Road broken by shellfire
- Hamlet/ruins

0 _____ 1,000yds
0 _____ 1,000m

After the bustle and barter of stores distribution, the men marched past the gun lines to the subway entrances or communications trenches. Traffic had to be painstakingly managed, as there was no room for two-way flow. The subways operated a traffic light system enforced by military police. Encumbered and anxious, the single files of men made clumsy passage through the darkness, tripping on duckboards, snagging on communications cable and bumping into each other. Once positioned in the cramped tunnels or trenches, they settled down as best they could, descending into their own thoughts.

The waiting felt interminable. Sleep was snatched and fitful, interrupted by cold, pins and needles or the kick of a passing messenger . Men talked, seeking answers from neighbours equally uncertain of their immediate future. In the dim light of weak bulbs, some were fidgeting, fingering weapons, and checking equipment incessantly. Others shared forced humour, played cards or etched graffiti into the chalk to evade nerves. At one point or another, most would have spared a thought for home and the circumstances that had conspired to put them into this predicament. No one was truly expecting to die – that was something that happened to other people – but they had seen enough of the front line to understand the dangers that lay ahead.

Contrary to what many might perceive, senior commanders were also pensive at this hour. Byng and his divisional commanders had made their plan. Now it was out of their hands. One can only imagine the weight of responsibility they felt as Z-Hour approached.

# THE BATTLE

### 'First a little rum, then blood ...'

Easter Sunday had been a relatively mild, dry day but in the early hours of Easter Monday, 9 April, the weather became cold and overcast. Around 0400hrs, the subway exits were opened and having had their customary rum ration and final mug of sweet tea, the leading assault waves filed

The company cook doles out the 'hash'. In rear areas, food was of a higher quality and the men had more time to eat it. The chefs made a special effort to give the men their last decent meal before moving up to assembly areas. Readers will be comforted to note that the containers in the foreground are still in use today. (IWM, CO 1288)

Scaling ladders being fixed to the British front line in Arras on 8 April 1917. Note that provision is being made for both directions. Many Canadian Battalions in the initial assault entered no man's land via tunnel exits blown especially for the purpose. This was less predictable than linear waves and suited current tactics. (IWM, Q6229)

noiselessly into no man's land. On the parapets of the Canadian front line, wire was pulled aside for other assault platoons and they clambered up the trench ladders and crawled forward into shell holes. Those final moments witnessed pats of encouragement and handshakes. By now, a grim determination was setting in. As one Canadian private recalled it, 'First a little rum, then blood ...'

Machine-gunners lay out the belts of ammunition on groundsheets and worked the greased parts backwards and forwards to check their function. In the rear areas, ground crews were preparing 16 Squadron BE2cs. On the battery positions, gunners pulled damp canvas tarpaulins off the ammunition stacks and slid the first rounds into the cold breeches. The Germans had been tetchy all night, sending up illumination flares and firing machine guns into no man's land. Now they too had quietened down.

A light sleet set in, dulling the hint of dawn behind the ridge. Watches had been synchronized but the attack was initiated by a signal gun in the centre of the line at 0530hrs precisely. It is said that every single artillery piece had its firing lanyard extended ready to react.

The men shivering in no man's land do not recall its report. Their first recollection was the shrill rush of shells passing overhead followed by the most unforgettable sight they would ever see. The entire length of the ridge just 100 yards to their front became a boiling, angry, tearing mass of explosions – each penetrating the gloom like lightning. Clods of chalk and timbers were raining down. To their flanks, the machine guns barked into life, the damp air reducing their report to a laboured slapping sound. They were barely audible above the din of barrage, which many described as a tangible 'ceiling of sound'. Lieutenant Bittlau, a German eyewitness with 263rd Infantry Regiment, described it this way:

> As if by command a barrage spat from large and small calibre mouths building to an unsurpassed frenzy of fire. The impact of each salvo is indistinguishable from the next ... Nerves are stretched to breaking point,

*drinking in this image, this beautiful terrifying painting. A pulsating beat in the left breast … the heart is like lead, it beats in the throat and stops the breathing. Blood surges into the mouth, sense fades away.*[14]

Desperate German signal rockets arced haphazardly into the sky from the German support line, calling for protective fires from the gun positions to the lee of the ridge. There was only a desultory response. Beyond the linear creeping barrage, the heavy guns were firing 'standing' barrages against German depth positions. McNaughton's counter-battery plan was initiated – gun positions being hit with a mix of high explosive and gas shells. His precise calculations paid dividends; all but *two* of *Gruppe Vimy's* 69 artillery batteries had been plotted accurately and were shelled that morning. As soon as it was light enough, 16 Squadron was in the air over the German rear areas, prioritizing counter-battery fires as the German guns attempted to react. This was a hazardous duty. A sky thick with passing shells buffeted the little planes. Pilots recall the hum and vibration of a near miss. 'Friendly' shells brought down three aircraft that day.

As planned, 'The Pimple', Hill 145, Les Tilleuls and Thelus were smoked off by trench mortars and gassed with heavier-than-air choking agents but only five of the 18 offensive mining projects reached fruition that morning. The mines that did blow were effective, particularly the three detonated to assist the 73rd Battalion on the extreme left of 4th Division where most of the German frontline garrison was killed outright. Nevertheless, a subsequent report by the Inspector of Mines declared: 'Mining did not play an important part in the action of 9th April.' This is slightly misleading as without the work of the tunnelling companies, none of the complex subway systems would have been complete. The offensive mines were abandoned for a number of reasons. One of the largest schemes, aimed at destroying German support line works on the north of the ridge, was just not finished in time. The galleries being driven towards 'The Pimple' were collapsed by

A German 5.9in. (15cm) howitzer destroyed by counter-battery fire in Farbus Wood. British soldiers nicknamed it the 'Jack Johnson' after a popular coloured boxer of the pre-war era because its shell was both destructive and left a thick pall of black smoke. It was also known as the 'coal box' for the same reason. Arguably, it was the most versatile and effective artillery piece of the entire war. (IWM, CO 2219)

the preparatory bombardment. Most often, work was suspended through fear of impeding the advance with yet more craters. This was a wise decision because the state of the ground was already appalling.

After three minutes, the barrage lifted on schedule and the guns elevated to fire 100m beyond. The infantry were already pressing forward. German outposts on crater lips were rushed as soon as the barrage opened. Battalions advanced with two companies 'up' and two in support. Within the companies, their four platoons did the same, attacking in linear waves two sections deep or in diamond shaped section groups called 'artillery formation'. The latter was designed for movement out of contact but in the twilight and stumbling through the shelled morass, it was more conducive to cohesion.

In the overwhelming majority of cases, progress to Black Line objectives was successful. Both 1st and 2nd Divisions had reported it by just 0615hrs. The creeping barrage on frontline trenches had pinned the defenders in their dugouts. Sentries, if alive, were stunned and easily overcome. Assaulting companies left the dugout entrances in the hands of specially tasked 'moppers' and pushed on to the next line with the barrage.

By this time, some second-line garrisons were already alerted and managing to reach their fire positions in time to organize resistance. Maxim guns were being brought into action; many from ad hoc mounts where concrete strongpoints had been destroyed by bombardment. Marksmen were also effective. War diaries refer to them as a 'nuisance' – somewhat of an understatement for the officers who were picked off with ruthless accuracy. The creeping barrage still managed to keep these engagements at close range, allowing platoons to deal with them in textbook fashion.

With the platoons drilled so well, advances were not held up long. The Lewis gun section went firm; gunner and assistant finding a stable firing position while the remainder broke open ammunition. Though not as reliable as the heavier Vickers, the Lewis gun performed well. Its

**Grange Crater looking north up the front line towards Hill 145. This photograph was taken in the 1920s but the dimensions of the mine crater are still clear. They posed a significant obstacle – the main reason why Byng abandoned the plan to blow 13 of his 18 mines on 9 April. (IWM, CO 1618)**

This destroyed German concrete strongpoint in the village of Thelus demonstrates the ferocity of the so-called 'Week of Suffering'. These machine-gun nests were the cornerstones of von Fasbender's defence of Vimy Ridge. Not all were destroyed in this manner but there was only limited redundancy. The bombardment levelled the odds for the asaulting infantry. (IWM, CO 1142)

The Arras–Lille road atop Vimy Ridge. We will have to take the photographer's word for it. The chalk fragments, buried concrete strongpoint and total eradication of the road is further evidence of the effect achieved by an entire army's scaling of heavy artillery in such a limited area. (IWM, CO 1145)

fat barrel housed a honeycombed air-cooling system, allowing a fair rate of fire from the 47-round drum magazines. Dependent on the scenario, the Lewis could either pin down the enemy being attacked or suppress deeper positions that threatened the assault. Rifle bombers would then find an oblique position such as a shell hole and fire salvoes of No. 36 Mills bombs from the cup dischargers on their .303in. Lee Enfield barrels. When practised, this provided a surprisingly effective barrage, allowing the section of bombers to work their way round to a flank and storm the objective. The reserve section of riflemen could be used in any number of ways – as a genuine uncommitted reserve element, for accurate suppression of the enemy, or as extra manpower for the assault. If the position were not adequately suppressed, assaulting forces would 'break down' into two parts, firing and dashing forward in a leapfrog motion.[15] In the confusion, close-quarters battle often became a duel between opposing bombers, lobbing grenades and snap shooting at fleeting glimpses of helmet.

When casualties took their toll, especially among junior leaders, the élan and training combined to produce some impressive acts of personal bravery. In 3rd Brigade of 1st Division, a company of the 16th Battalion was held up by machine-gun fire on the second line. When the platoon attack lost momentum, Private William Milne crawled forward and silenced it single-handed with grenades, killing the crew and capturing the weapon. A Scottish-born emigrant recruited in Moose Jaw, British Columbia, he was awarded the Victoria Cross. Sadly, it was a posthumous decoration because he was killed later that day.

Some planners had worried that the three-minute barrage schedule for each 100m was too cautious. In light of the skirmishes, glutinous mud and deep shell holes, it proved well judged.

Up in 3rd Division's area, the advance to Black Line objectives was less eventful. Leading platoons did not recognize the German first line trenches. All that was left after bombardment was a chalky depression, soft and smoking underfoot. Any German troops in dugouts on this line had been entombed. As their official account puts it, 'these hours were a rich harvest for Death'.[16]

The Germans holding this part of the line were from the 79th Reserve Infantry Division. 3rd Division's attack was centred on the boundary between the 262nd and 263rd Reserve Infantry Regiments, commanded by Major Freiherr von Rotenhan and Oberleutnant von Behr respectively. In reaction to the lack of depth on their part of the ridge, they took the unorthodox step of fighting two battalions forward as opposed to one behind the other. This was also in part due to the woeful undermanning across the division. Some companies mustered as few as 60 men, though the average among the regiments was between 120 and 150. As described previously, these were good troops and well prepared but they were overwhelmed this day. The front-loading of their dispositions led to half the force being killed or captured in the first hour. One lesson this battle identified for the German high command was the folly of putting entire companies into one dugout. 1st Battalion, The Canadian Mounted Regiment (CMR), on the extreme right of 3rd

Canadians guarding German dugout entrances. The overhead protection is designed to prevent the entrances from becoming blocked by shellfire. In many cases, men were entombed and across Vimy Ridge, the Germans paid a high price for placing so many men into single dugouts. (IWM, CO 1154)

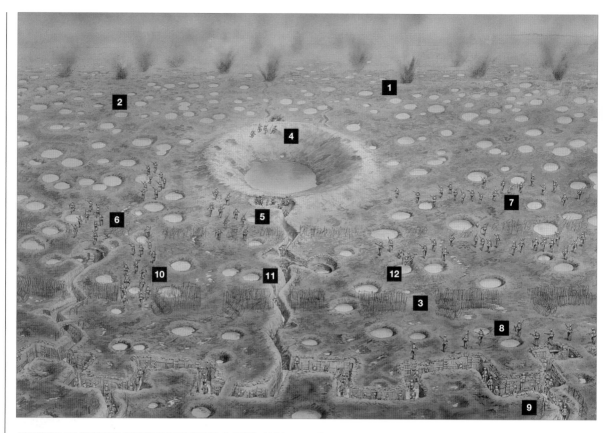

## ADVANCE OF THE 2ND CANADIAN DIVISION, 9 APRIL 1917
(pages 58–59)

Canadian infantry from 19th Battalion, 4th Brigade, 2nd Canadian Division, advance under a creeping barrage at 0535hrs on Easter Monday, 9 April 1917. The depiction is somewhat contrived in order to illustrate a number of aspects of the battle but nevertheless it captures the essence of the scene. It was considerably darker at that time and the trenches in the foreground are in better repair than the actual examples would have been but both concessions to clarity improve the perspective. The traversing, revetment and outpost positions are well represented, in particular the post holding the lip of the mine crater in the centre of the illustration. Craters were less common on this southern area of the ridge than further north and akin to this example, dated back to the mining campaigns of 1916 – hence the settled chalk spoil and pond at the base. The infantry attacked under the protection of a 'creeping barrage' and the dirty smudges of the 18-pdr. shell detonations are faithfully recreated here (1). Sheet flame and spectacular explosions are the preserve of Hollywood, flashes from shell detonations being more or less instantaneous. Note the accompanying smoke and dust, known in the military as 'obscuration'. Assaulting troops kept as close to this barrage as possible, in this case between 75 and 100m. The destruction of German barbed wire entanglements by preparatory phases of the barrage plan was complete and the shattered pickets are just visible forward of the German front line (2). Note how the Canadian wire has been pulled aside to form lanes through which they can advance (3). A Canadian half section is capturing the German outpost at the far lip of the crater and they are clearing it with grenades (4). A Vickers machine-gun section has set up on the nearside and is assisting with the suppression of German front-line defences as the attackers press forward. (5) This scene demonstrates both ways in which infantry platoons advanced in 1917 and should be examined in conjunction with the Tactics Pamphlet extract on page 37. To the left, the platoon is adopting 'Artillery Formation' (6). These tight section groupings assisted control and cohesion and though usually favoured out of contact with the enemy, were used in the assault where darkness and confusion may have precluded the more open and conventional linear pattern evident on the right. In the latter instance, the platoon is advancing with its rifle and reserve sections to the front, supported by the rifle-grenade section rear left and Lewis-gun section rear right (7). 'Artillery Formation' is similar but the diamond shape places the rifle grenades abreast of the reserve with the rifle section in the lead. In both cases, platoon headquarters is arranged in the centre, where control can best be maintained. 'Moppers' are seen exiting the trenches on the right, ready to support the advance of the lead platoons (8) and follow-on waves remain protected in the front line until it is their turn to assume the advance (9). In the Lewis-gun sections, men can be seen carrying the panniers containing extra ammunition drums (10) and a party bearing ammunition for the Vickers section is shown making its way up the communications trench to the crater outpost (11). The pockmarked, muddy ground was laborious to cross and one man in the right-hand platoon has already become stuck in a shell hole (12). (Illustration by Peter Dennis)

Division captured a company of 150 men from 3rd Battalion, 263rd Regiment, in a dugout on the second line.

At the northern end, 4th Division also struck a boundary, this time between two *Gruppen* – the 16th Bavarian Division of *Gruppe Souchez* and the 79th Reserve Infantry Division of *Gruppe Vimy*. The latter held Hill 145 with the 261st Reserve Infantry Regiment under Oberst Wilhelm von Goerne. With his sector just 1km deep, he also fought two battalions forward.

Major-General David Watson reconfigured his brigades; splitting 10th Brigade down and bolstering each assaulting brigade – 11th and 12th – with the 47th and 46th Battalions respectively. The balance of 10th Brigade (44th and 50th Battalions) awaited the planned attack on 'The Pimple' the next day.

12th Brigade had the most limited of all Canadian Corps objectives. On its extreme left, the 73rd Battalion were tasked with capturing the first two German trenches in order to taper the Canadian advance with I Corps on the defensive at Souchez. This was a suitable opportunity for the application of offensive mining and three were blown, killing the Germans in the front line outright. It was a pretty instantaneous death for most, just a brief, violent rumbling to presage the event.[17]

After such a terrifying display of firepower, the majority of the second line garrison fled towards Givenchy below. Lewis gun and rifle fire ensured that most did not reach its sanctuary. One report described them as 'executed'.

Further up the front, 72nd and 38th Battalions were advancing in like fashion but with deeper objectives. They too made good progress over the first line but could not keep up with the barrage when pushing on to the second. The defending Bavarians opposing the 72nd emerged from their dugouts and initiated a withering fire. Quick-thinking company commanders took cover, put down a base of fire and sent entire platoons round the southern flank (under the protection of the 73rd) to bomb their way up the trench. The 38th were not so fortunate with the ground. They struggled through a frontal assault against the right battalion of 261st Regiment, some wounded men drowning in flooded shell holes. On reaching the Black line, they were exhausted and consolidated there. It was to be a hideous day. When relieved, only 60 men out of 700 answered roll call.

11th Brigade fared even worse. With 1km² of the ridge, Brigadier-General Odlum was able to concentrate his six available battalions into two double waves with the 85th and 47th in reserve. On his right, he led with the 102nd Battalion, backed up by the 75th. The 102nd crested the hill in similar vein to their 3rd Division neighbours and were preparing to exploit all the way to the Red Line. The disaster unfolded on their left.

Major Harry Shaw, commanding officer of the 87th Battalion (Canadian Grenadier Guards), had made a specific request that the artillery desist from bombarding the German first line. Given that it lay just 150m away, he was confident of taking it and wanted it intact for the purposes of consolidation. The decision cost him fifty per cent casualties in just 60 seconds. The forward German company was waiting on the parapet. After six minutes, when the barrage lifted off the second line, the supporting Maxims joined in, pinning down the supporting 75th

# THE ASSAULT ON VIMY RIDGE

9 April 1917, attack of the Canadian Corps 1st and 2nd Infantry Divisions viewed from the south.

Note: Gridlines are shown at intervals of ½ mile/.80 km.

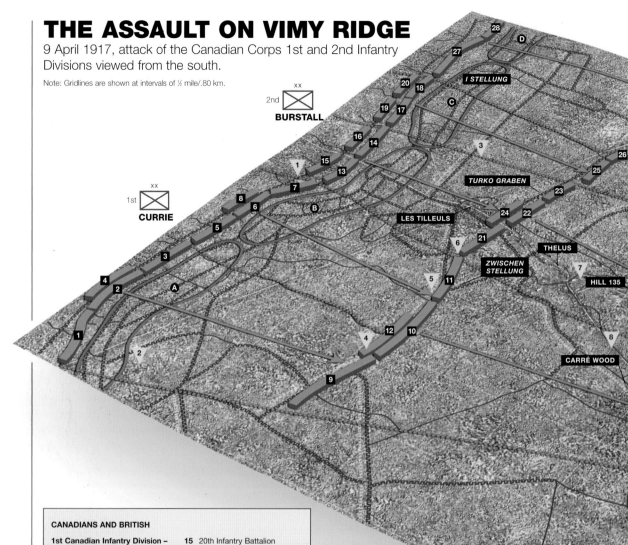

**CANADIANS AND BRITISH**

**1st Canadian Infantry Division –**
**Major-General Currie**

*2nd Canadian Infantry Brigade –*
*Brigadier-General Loomis*
1   5th Infantry Battalion
2   7th Infantry Battalion
3   10th Infantry Battalion
4   8th Infantry Battalion

*3rd Canadian Infantry Brigade –*
*Brigadier-General Tuxford*
5   15th Infantry Battalion
6   14th Infantry Battalion
7   16th Infantry Battalion
8   13th Infantry Battalion

*1st Canadian Infantry Brigade –*
*Brigadier-General Griesbach*
9   1st Infantry Battalion
10  3rd Infantry Battalion
11  4th Infantry Battalion
12  2nd Infantry Battalion

**2nd Canadian Infantry Division**
**– Major-General Burstall**

*4th Canadian Infantry Brigade –*
*Brigadier-General Rennie*
13  18th Infantry Battalion
14  19th Infantry Battalion

15  20th Infantry Battalion
16  21st Infantry Battalion

*5th Canadian Infantry Brigade –*
*Brigadier-General MacDonell*
17  24th Infantry Battalion
18  26th Infantry Battalion
19  22nd Infantry Battalion
20  25th Infantry Battalion

*6th Canadian Infantry Brigade –*
*Brigadier-General Ketchen*
21  31st Infantry Battalion
22  28th Infantry Battalion
23  29th Infantry Battalion
24  27th Infantry Battalion

*13th Infantry Brigade (British 5th*
*Infantry Division) – Brigadier-*
*General Jones*
25  1st Battalion Royal West
    Kents (British)
26  2nd Battalion King's Own
    Scottish Borderers (British)

27  8th Infantry Brigade, 3rd
    Canadian Infantry Division
28  7th Infantry Brigade, 3rd
    Canadian Division

**GERMANS**

*1st Bavarian Reserve Infantry Division –*
*Major-General von Bechmann*
A  Bavarian Reserve Infantry Regiment No. 1
B  Bavarian Reserve Infantry Regiment No. 3

*79th Reserve Infantry Division – Major-General*
*von Bacmeister*
C  Reserve Infantry Regiment No. 263
D  Reserve Infantry Regiment No. 262

German Artillery
E  79th Res. Infantry Division Field Artillery
   Brigade Positions
F  1st Bav. Res. Infantry Division Field Artillery
   Brigade Positions

## ▼ EVENTS

**1. 0530HRS:** **Zero Hour. Creeping barrage and indirect machine-gun fire opens across corps frontage. First waves assault German front line.**

**2. 0600HRS:** **Both divisions making good progress but 19th Battalion and 5th Battalion held up by stay-behind machine-gun nests.**

**3. 0720HRS:** **4th and 5th Brigades report Black Line objectives taken on schedule. The frontline battalion of 79th Division, Regt. No. 263, boasted only one survivor.**

**4. 0730HRS:** **Bavarian Reserve Infantry Regiment No. 3 in full retreat towards Farbus. Raked by Vickers machine-gun fire and light artillery, only 200 men from the two battalions in the line survived.**

**5. 0825HRS:** **2nd and 3rd Brigades report Black Line objectives taken.**

**6. 0930HRS:** ***Zwischenstellung*** **(Red Line objective) consolidated. 1st, 6th and 13th Brigades ready to resume advance after planned 90-minute pause in the barrage.**

**7. 1040HRS:** **Thelus captured by 28th and 31st Battalions, 6th Brigade. Having been subjected to a concerted bombardment, it was burning heavily. The accompanying smoke helped screen the Canadian advance from undestroyed machine guns on Hill 135.**

**8. 1115HRS:** **1st Brigade reports capture of Blue Line objectives. 6th and 13th Brigades report Blue Line objectives secure at 1130hrs. Not one of the eight tanks allocated to 2nd Division made it as far as the Blue Line.**

**9. 1225HRS:** **1st Brigade commence advance onto Brown Line objectives (Farbus Wood) despite enfilading fire from objectives not taken by the 51st Highland Division to the south.**

**10. 1330HRS:** **1st Brigade troops in Farbus Wood and probing beyond.**

**11. 1450HRS:** **Germans reported to be retiring from Farbus and its woods to *II Stellung*. An improvised defensive line is based around the railway embankment.**

**12. 1620HRS:** **Two troop-strength patrols from the Canadian Light Horse set off for Willerval. By 1700hrs both patrols have been driven back with heavy casualties. Out of 35 cavalrymen, only two return on their mounts.**

BONVAL WOOD
(also referred to as La Folie Wood)

T'S WOOD

GOULOT WOOD

VIMY

TOWN WOOD
(also referred to as
La Bois de la Ville)

*II STELLUNG*

FARBUS

STATION WOOD

E

10

FARBUS WOOD

F

MANDANT'S
HOUSE

LONG WOOD

WILLERVAL

B

79th Res. XX

**VON BACMEISTER**

1st Bav.
Res. XX

**VON BECHMANN**

N

**63**

Troops from the 87th Battalion (Canadian Grenadier Guards) messing. This battalion had a disastrous morning on 9 April, owing to their request not to bombard the front line opposing them. Their fate was a chilling demonstration of what might have occurred across the corps if the artillery preparation had not been so comprehensive. (IWM, CO 1706)

Battalion in their assembly trenches. It was mayhem reminiscent of the Somme. The determined Grenadiers pressed on in small bands, with some making it past the first line. This confused the battle picture with reports that they were making headway. Odlum never received any word either way. The 54th Battalion advanced to relieve the 102nd and take Red objectives. Instead they were scythed in the flank by enfilade fire from the centre and forced to withdraw. In 12th Brigade on the left, the 78th Battalion was due to do the same for the 38th. They too were struck in the flank. By this time, the smoke was clearing from 'The Pimple'. Two Maxim guns opened up immediately, harassing both the 78th and the 72nd Battalion in the centre.

By 0700hrs, 4th Division was in a mess. Most of the battalions had left their trenches. Communications were reliant on runners – many of whom were not making it back unscathed. The artillery could not break the impasse because the 102nd and 38th Battalions were too far forward.

Fortunately, these setbacks were confined to less than a mile of front. Elsewhere the other three divisions were experiencing unprecedented success. On 3rd Division's front, the 40-minute barrage pause at the Black Line expired and at Z plus 75, they were off again. The foul weather and lack of landmarks caused some battalions to stray off axis, but resistance was not sufficient to capitalize on the confusion. The mighty *Zwischenstellung* was taken in a bound and 2nd Battalion CMR pushed through the rubble of La Folie Farm without incident. By 0730hrs, the division was cresting Vimy Ridge and approaching their limit of exploitation, La Folie Wood. The machine-gun detachments were among the first to arrive and established positions with good arcs down the slope. Across the corps effort, 130 Vickers guns were apportioned to the consolidation effort. The official German account recalls their potency as a battalion staff tried to withdraw:

> *About 200m south-west from the abandoned fire trenches* [I Stellung], *the first English were appearing … who had brought into position … a machine gun whose monotone melody cackled incessantly from here on. Hotly pursued by fire from this troublesome machine gun in the midst of*

A reserve brigade makes its way forward to the Red Line. This photograph conveys the desolation of Vimy Ridge in 1917, something very difficult to imagine when one visits today. (IWM, CO 1155)

*artillery fire raging directly over Vimy village, the staff hurried to the Zwischenstellung in almost knee-deep mud. Besides the Adjutant, the Signals officer, both orderlies and three radio operators were lost.*[18]

On the boundary between 7th and 8th Brigade, 4th Battalion CMR and The Royal Canadian Regiment were embroiled in the stumps of an old orchard, beating off section-strength counter-attacks by determined Saxons from the rear companies of 2nd Battalion, 262nd Regiment. Nor was that the only hindrance. Owing to the problems on Hill 145, the 42nd Battalion (Canadian Black Watch) on the boundary with 4th Division was receiving increasing quantities of enfilade fire. Brigadier-General A. C. Macdonnell commanding 7th Brigade was forced to order the 42nd to come out of the line and prepare a defensive position perpendicular to their axis, protecting the exposed flank. It was a costly mission and they sustained 200 casualties in the course of the next four hours. The PPCLI shifted left to fill in on the Red Line limit of exploitation as carrying parties arrived from the reserve battalions to assist with consolidation.

Having resumed their own advance from the Black Line at about 0645hrs, both 1st and 2nd Divisions had no comparable difficulties taking Red line objectives. 4th Brigade of 2nd Division launched its follow-on battalions, the 20th and 21st. They had the hamlet of Les

German captives being processed rearwards. They were allowed to keep greatcoats and ration utensils as well as helmets. There was a good reason for this. With German shelling being haphazard and belated, quite a few prisoners suffered at the hands of their own artillery. (IWM, CO 1193)

Tilleuls to deal with. It formed the nub of a complicated X-shaped switch between the *Zwischenstellung* and *Turko Graben* German trench systems. Its shattered state compounded the complications but akin to 3rd Division's hiccup, the Prussian and Bavarian defenders at this crucial junction were in no fit state to take advantage. The 2nd Division reached the Red Line from approximately 0800hrs.

Currie's 1st Division fared even better. On the Black Line, support waves of the lead battalions resumed the advance. It is claimed that lead elements were onto the Red Line by 0700hrs, but this is debatable. Even so, 1st Brigade was not in a position to resume the advance until 0925hrs when the barrage was also due to end its pause and proceed. Many accounts of the battle seem to

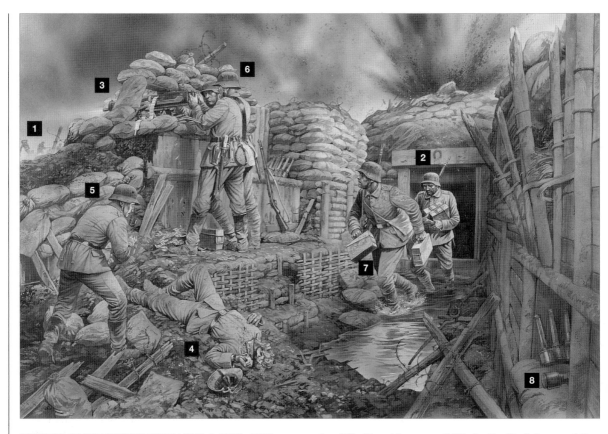

**DEFENCE OF THE *ZWISCHENSTELLUNG*, 9 APRIL 1917**
(pages 66–67)

A Maxim machine-gun section from 5th Company, 2nd Battalion, 261st Prussian Infantry Regiment, defends the front line on Hill 145, 0600hrs Easter Monday, 9 April 1917. This illustration captures the urgency and intensity of the battle for that part of Vimy Ridge. Opposing this company was the 87th Infantry Battalion (Canadian Grenadier Guards) from 11th Brigade of Canadian 4th Division. They had opted not to destroy a portion of the German front line, most likely because they wanted it preserved for the purposes of consolidation. Consequently, when the attack was launched, the Prussian defenders were able to bring their machine guns to bear and decimate the assaulting Canadians. These troops are just visible to the left of the picture (1). A six-man section under a junior non-commissioned officer (NCO) served the Maxim gun. A more senior officer (probably the company or battalion commander) would have sited it but the NCO was responsible for its local defence, ammunition supply and rate of fire once in action. During the preparatory bombardment, the section took shelter in a deep dugout (2) and emerged at the last safe moment. The Maxim gun went below with them and was carried up on its sledge mount and set in the pre-prepared emplacement in a well-rehearsed, slick manoeuvre. In this instance, the trench has sustained a degree of damage from the creeping barrage, weakening the revetment and collapsing the fire step on the left (3). It is waterlogged from months of inclement winter weather. The NCO section commander has already been killed by a shrapnel wound to the left of his head (4). Given his responsibility for the Maxim's arcs of fire, he was compelled to look over the parapet, a duty he has paid the price for. An ammunition orderly, his unlit pipe still clamped in his teeth by force of habit, looks on with alarm (5). The next most senior man was the 'Number One' firing the gun with his 'Number Two' keeping it fed with ammunition. The 'Number Two' was also responsible for keeping the weapon cool, a major consideration during a battle of this intensity (6). The Maxim relied on a water-cooled system (contained in the 'jacket' around the barrel), which was actually more effective than later air-cooled systems, but much more cumbersome as a consequence. The remaining members of the section keep busy ferrying and preparing ammunition boxes (7). Ammunition supply is the chief limitation on the effectiveness of a machine gun with its 500 rounds per minute rate of fire. In a static position like this, it is manageable because large amounts can be pre-positioned. In the advance, it is much more of a challenge and commanders must enforce strict expenditure discipline. Dotted around the position are stocks of stick grenades to keep assaulting infantry at bay (8). The close-quarters battles over strongpoints like this one often degenerated into a stand-off duel between bombing parties and generally were settled by acts of conspicuous gallantry from one side or the other. 5th Company held out for six hours until they were eventually overcome by the remnants of the 87th Infantry Battalion who clawed their way forward. With just two Maxim sections left in action, their tenacity and courage in the face of such odds must not go unrecognised.(Illustration by Peter Dennis)

The 28th Battalion Signals Detachment. Of particular interest is the air marker panel in the background, which has been placed out in response to the klaxon call of a passing 16 Squadron RFC contact patrol. (IWM, CO 1165)

disregard the role of the creeping and standing barrages after 0530hrs. This does the gunners no justice. They laboured hard all morning to sustain a timely and dense barrage to protect the advance. Even when the term 'pause' is used, the barrage did not cease. It screened the forward passage of lines with a depth barrage at about half the available guns, while the remainder organized themselves for the next push.

A change in wind direction to the south also assisted 1st Division. The smoke lingering over Thelus was cast in front of the defending Bavarians, adding an impromptu screen to the effects of barrage. At about 0730hrs, an entire battalion was spotted withdrawing east towards Farbus Wood. This explains the relative ease with which 1st Brigade exploited onto the Blue and Brown Lines later. Given the situation on that part of the ridge, wholesale retreat was understandable. Both the forward lines and *Zwischenstellung* had fallen without any delay. A concerted and accurate barrage preceded the advance with no guns available to retaliate. The men were exhausted, hungry and outflanked by Canadian gains on the narrower front to their north. One would have admired a determined stand for its tenacity but not for its wisdom.

At about the same time as this withdrawal, the first of the 16 Squadron contact patrols came over, sounding klaxons as a signal for the Canadian battalions to lay out the air marker panels. The klaxons were a novel way of preventing battalions from laying out marker panels on the appearance of aircraft tasked with other duties, such as artillery fire adjustment. One 16 Squadron aircraft on that duty spotted an enemy battery of 5.9in. howitzers attempting to limber up and withdraw. In its improvised strafing run the plane managed to wound some horses, tangling the limber and preventing further retreat. Advancing troops from 1st Brigade later captured the battery.

Back up on the northern end of the battle, 78th Battalion had reached their Red Line objectives through sheer bloody-mindedness. That effort did not leave much energy or manpower for an effective consolidation and at 0830hrs they were subjected to counter-attack.

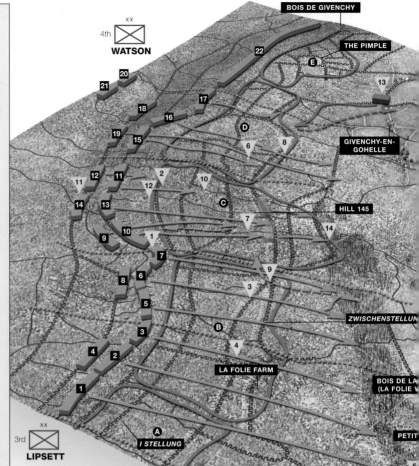

## CANADIANS AND BRITISH

**3rd Canadian Infantry Division –**
**Major-General Lipsett**

*8th Canadian Infantry Brigade –*
*Brigadier-General Elmsley*
1   1st Battalion Canadian Mounted Rifles
2   2nd Battalion Canadian Mounted Rifles
3   4th Battalion Canadian Mounted Rifles
4   5th Battalion Canadian Mounted Rifles

*7th Canadian Infantry Brigade –*
*Brigadier-General Macdonnell*
5   The Royal Canadian Regiment
6   Princess Patricia's Canadian Light Infantry
7   42nd Infantry Battalion (Canadian Black
    Watch)
8   49th Infantry Battalion

**4th Canadian Infantry Division –**
**Major-General Watson**

*11th Canadian Infantry Brigade –*
*Brigadier-General Odlum*
9    54th Infantry Battalion
10   102nd Infantry Battalion
11   87th Infantry Battalion
12   75th Infantry Battalion
13   85th Infantry Battalion
14   47th Infantry Battalion (detached from 10th
     Brigade)

*12th Canadian Infantry Brigade –*
*Brigadier-General MacBrian*
15   38th Infantry Battalion
16   72nd Infantry Battalion
17   73rd Infantry Battalion
18   78th Infantry Battalion
19   48th Infantry Battalion (detached from 10th
     Brigade)

*10th Canadian Infantry Brigade –*
*Brigadier-General Hilliam*
20   44th Infantry Battalion
21   50th Infantry Battalion

Flanking Units to North
22   13th Battalion The Middlesex Regiment,
     73rd British Infantry Brigade (24th Division)

## ▼ EVENTS

1. **0530HRS:** **Zero Hour. Creeping barrage and indirect machine-gun fire opens across corps frontage. First waves assault German front line.**

2. **0600HRS:** **11th Brigade, 4th Division, experiencing mixed fortunes. 102nd Battalion making fair progress on the right, but further north the 87th taking casualties reminiscent of the Somme.**

3. **0625HRS:** **3rd Division lead waves report Black Line objectives secure, making such good progress that some lead companies blunder into their own protective barrage.**

4. **0700HRS:** **The Saxons' tenacious defence in the shattered orchards north of La Folie Farm hampers the Royal Canadian Regiment on right flank of 7th Brigade. Local counter-attacks are bold but ineffective.**

5. **0730HRS:** **8th Brigade of 3rd Division exploits all the way to Red Line objectives. Their centre battalion, the 2nd Canadian Mounted Regiment, captures La Folie Farm en route. When complete on their limit of exploitation, the brigade starts to consolidate the western edge of La Folie Wood.**

6. **0745HRS:** **12th Brigade making fairly tortuous progress up to Black Line objectives. 38th and 72nd Battalions taking casualties from both enfilade fire on the uncaptured Hill 145 to their south and pockets of Germans emerging from undamaged dugouts.**

7. **0800HRS:** **11th Brigade now in grave disorder. 87th all but wiped out, 75th pinned down in Canadian frontline trenches. The 102nd Battalion on the summit but reduced to two companies under the command of a corporal. 54th Battalion behind them is decimated from its open flank and forced to withdraw.**

8. **0830HRS:** **78th Battalion of 12th Brigade passes through the exhausted 38th Battalion and pushes on to gain a tenuous hold on Red Line objectives. 72nd Battalion is holding its Red Line objectives under pressure from 'The Pimple' to the north. 73rd Battalion on extreme left flank is doing good work holding the integrity of the line.**

9. **0900HRS:** **With 4th Division being repulsed from Hill 145, Brig. Gen. Macdonnell orders the 42nd Battalion to prepare positions protecting the exposed northern flank. The PPCLI stretch to fill the vacated line on La Folie Wood.**

10. **1030HRS:** **4th Division front 'settled' into a salient bulging back towards the Canadian original front line. Intrepid survivors from 87th and 102nd cling to the gains they made and repel local counter-attacks.**

11. **1450HRS:** **Amidst the confusion, a forlorn Brigadier Odlum gambles on the 85th Battalion and issues orders for a dusk attack onto Hill 145.**

12. **1845HRS:** **Without barrage, the 85th throw themselves at the ridge with extraordinary fortitude and drive the German 261st Regiment survivors out of the salient, balancing 11th Brigade's line on Black Line objectives.**

13. **2000HRS:** **In an attempt to recapture Hill 145's summit, a reserve battalion from 16th Bavarian Infantry Division fashion a counter-attack from Givenchy but it falters in the darkness without cohesion.**

14. **10 APRIL, 1515HRS:** **The two uncommitted 10th Brigade Battalions, 50th and 44th, attack from consolidated Black Line objectives on Hill 145 and rout the remaining German defenders off the ridge. By 1700hrs, Red objectives are secure across the 4th Division frontage.**

# THE FIGHT FOR HILL 145 AND 'THE PIMPLE'

9 and 10 April 1917, attack of the Canadian Corps 3rd and 4th Infantry Divisions viewed from the south.

Note: Gridlines are shown at intervals of ½ mile/.80 km.

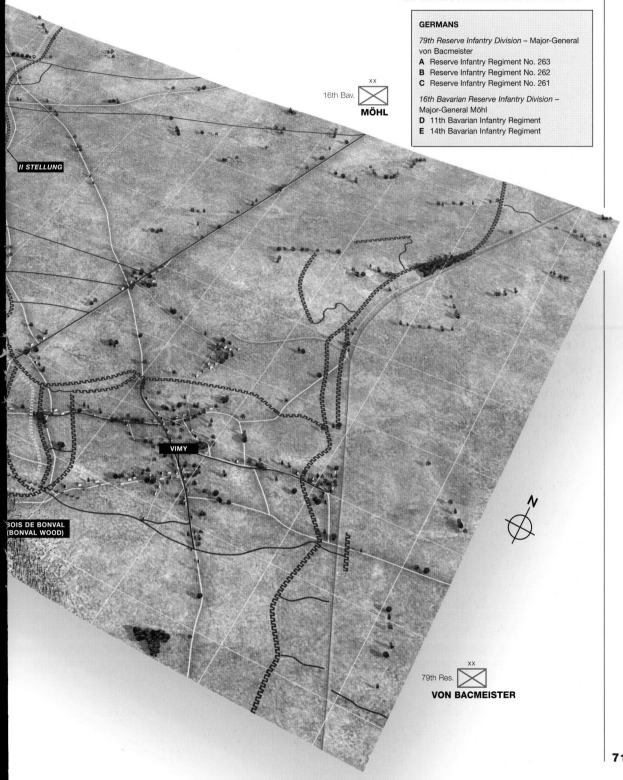

GERMANS

*79th Reserve Infantry Division* – Major-General von Bacmeister
**A** Reserve Infantry Regiment No. 263
**B** Reserve Infantry Regiment No. 262
**C** Reserve Infantry Regiment No. 261

*16th Bavarian Reserve Infantry Division* – Major-General Möhl
**D** 11th Bavarian Infantry Regiment
**E** 14th Bavarian Infantry Regiment

16th Bav. **MÖHL**

II STELLUNG

VIMY

BOIS DE BONVAL (BONVAL WOOD)

79th Res. **VON BACMEISTER**

The *Zwischenstellung* being improved in 3rd Division's area. In places the barrage had reduced it to a shallow depression and the Canadians took it in a bound, the defenders still sheltering in their dugouts. The foreground of this image provides an excellent example of the effect of bombardment on barbed wire. (IWM, CO 1167)

The German account of Vimy Ridge attests to a paucity of control and communication. For them it was very much a platoon and section commander's battle likened to an attempt at stemming an incoming tide – whatever obstacles they placed in the way were enveloped and eventually washed over. The bravery of these pockets of resistance has to be acknowledged, even if the detail of their exploits often died with them. In terms of the counter-attack against the 78th Battalion, we know that number 2 Company of 261st Regiment, led by Lieutenant Hoppe and supported by Maxims from the divisional specialist machine-gun detachments, was successful in driving the 78th back to the Black Line but could not achieve any more. Hasty company-level consolidations had afforded those positions sufficient integrity to resist.

Meanwhile, back on Hill 145, the remnants of the 87th Battalion were seriously demoralized. When history relates that they clung on, managing to form small bombing parties to capture the first line, it is worth taking the time to consider the courage that such an act demanded. The experience of the men pinned down up there is virtually indescribable. The survivors were freezing and covered in slime, their fingers swollen from cold, their canvas equipment stiff and restrictive. By now it was light. Two Maxim guns were working no man's land in this sector. Imagine a 19-year-old private sheltering alone in the cover of a shell hole. Every ten seconds or so, the methodical traverse swept his position, some rounds snapping over, others clipping the lip of his hole and showering him in mud and grit. Beyond view were the cries of leaders, flat bass crump of grenades and the haunting screams of wounded. He would have already seen his friends cut down in a heap, some mutilated beyond recognition. Men of a ghostly pallor lying in their own entrails, others clutching shattered limbs feebly. Worst of all were the head and facial injuries – brains blown out and jaws shot away. His officer was almost certainly a casualty. Fear turns a man into an empty vessel – he would not have anticipated this outcome. Numbed by revulsion and curled up in a ball, men in this state were being found by equally pale and dishevelled corporals. They were persuading these terrified strays to follow, to take on the 'Heinie'[19] with grenades – to do what the officers trained them to do.

By 1030hrs, a fairly stable salient had formed in the 4th Division line with the 78th Battalion on the left firm on Black objectives, 87th Battalion decimated and clinging to the first line in the centre, and 102nd Battalion holding Black Line objectives on the right. 3rd Division was securing the right flank by virtue of its advance to the Red Line.

### The green fields beyond

When 3rd Division consolidated on the western edge of Bois de la Folie, they were the first Canadian infantry to glimpse the Douai plain beyond Vimy Ridge. In astonishing contrast to the barren morass of chalky mud and shattered tree stumps they had struggled over, the plain stretched away before them, verdant and cultivated. In the distance they could see red-roofed miners' cottages and the slag heaps of the Lens coalfields. Indeed, the vista only alluded to the presence of war on account of the battered remnants of Vimy village and German gun limbers in full flight.

To their south, 1st and 2nd Divisions still had 2 to 3km of ground to capture. After a 90-minute pause, their advance beyond the Red Line re-opened at 0935hrs precisely. The 1st Division boundaries narrowed to a front of just 1km so they were able to attack with a single formation – Brigadier-General Griesbach's 1st Brigade. In contrast, 2nd Division's front widened towards the Blue and Brown lines, hence the attachment of Brigadier-General Jones' British 13th Brigade from 5th Division. They were to strike towards Goulot Wood over the northern crest of Hill 135 with 2nd Division's own 6th Brigade taking Thelus, Thelus Wood and Bois de Ville as their Blue and Brown objectives. Both 2nd Division brigades also had the *Zwischenstellung* to contend with in their attack frontage; it ran 500m east of the Red Line.

Right on the corps boundary with XVII Corps' 51st Highland Division, 1st Division also had a portion of the *Zwischenstellung* to capture because 2nd Brigade had stopped short of their Red objectives. 1st Battalion achieved this within just half an hour and 125 dazed Bavarians emerged in the wake of the barrage to make their way into captivity. 1st Brigade met remarkably light resistance en route to the Blue Line – principally in view of the support battalion's 0730hrs withdrawal. Some shellfire came in at

**Canadians of the 2nd Division advancing across Black Line objectives past a Mark II tank. The vehicle is almost certainly a bogged casualty of the opening phase as these infantrymen are far too relaxed to be the assaulting wave supported by armour. (IWM, CO 1575)**

'The Pimple' as viewed from the perspective of the 37th and 78th Battalions on 9 April. Its machine guns were able to enfilade the 72nd and 73rd Battalions advancing across the middle distance of the photograph from left to right. *I Stellung* front line positions are shown in red. (Author's collection)

random and inflicted light casualties but it was not sufficient to impose any delay. Lead companies hit Blue Line at 1130hrs and it had been consolidated and reported as taken by midday.

2nd Division's progress to the Blue Line was not quite as straight-forward. Planners had foreseen a tough battle for Thelus, which is one of the reasons tanks were deployed. They were supposed to invest the village and cover the clearance by Brigadier-General Ketchen's 6th Brigade. Of the eight tanks that started, one broke down on the start line, three more became bogged down or suffered mechanical failure in no man's land west of the Black Line, three met the same fate in and around Les Tilleuls and the last was destroyed by a direct hit from a German 5.9in. howitzer short of the Red Line. This did not discourage the 31st and 28th Battalions tasked with capturing Thelus. The carefully rehearsed clearance of the trench systems running parallel to its main street encountered negligible resistance. The brigade also took the *Zwischenstellung* (known here as Thelus trench) in their stride and were onto the Blue Line by 1115hrs.

To the north, the British 13th Brigade opened their advance with a similarly well-choreographed capture of the *Zwischenstellung*. In his report after the event, Brigadier-General Jones put this down to: 'The intensity and accuracy of the barrage put up by the Canadian artillery' and 'to previous practice over the taped course, which all commanders state was of immense assistance.'

From this point, Jones' left lead battalion – the 2nd King's Own Scottish Borderers (KOSB) – entered Goulot Wood at its northern end and cleared it to the south, cutting across the brigade advance. Jones had chosen this axis in preference to a frontal assault, as he feared the wood might be infested with dugouts and gun positions. It was a wise plan but they came under accurate sniper fire from the Bois de Bonval in 3rd Division's area to the north. Technically, this wood should have been cleared at this stage but 3rd Division did not report Red Line consolidated until midday. At any rate, one company was sent to bomb the dugouts. This they did with complete success. Goulot Wood

A dump of empty 18-pdr. shells at an ammunition distribution point behind the gun lines. Each 18-pdr. gun was stocked with 700 rounds before the battle started. One battery supporting 2nd Division reported over 600 rounds fired per gun between 0530hrs and 1300hrs. That was not atypical. (IWM, CO 1368)

represented the KOSB's Blue Line objective and limit of exploitation. It was reached at approximately 1130hrs.

As planned, there was a delay of 90 minutes at the Blue Line before the advance resumed to both divisions' final objective – the Brown Line. Across the entire ridge south-east of Hill 135, there were thick belts of wire between 20 and 50m thick. These were in place to protect the gun positions in Bois de Ville and Farbus Wood and ran oblique to the corps' axis. In order to meet this obstacle head on (and therefore shorten the length of any lanes cut through it), all three brigades would have to swing left, hinging on the KOSB consolidating Goulot Wood. The manoeuvre was complicated by the fact that some planned lanes through the wire were left undamaged by bombardment, necessitating the use of wire cutters. Furthermore, the creeping barrage was thinning as the advance outranged the rear field batteries.

At 1300hrs 13th Brigade swept down Goulot Wood led by the Royal West Kents, while 6th and 1st Brigades wheeled left behind the creeping barrage that adjusted its line in graduated sections. With well-rehearsed precision, the assaulting battalions descended onto the pre-cut lanes, improving them by hand where necessary. Breaching wire obstacles with cutters was an incredibly laborious and frustrating activity. In places, the belts were as dense as a bramble bush. Men were cut, snagged and tangled. Nevertheless, they made it through and pushed on towards the battery positions beyond.

The wire-cutting exercise had put the men in extremely bad humour so when the German batteries decided to fire over open sights at point-blank range, they got no quarter. After a quick salvo of rifle grenades to suppress the protecting machine guns, the artillerymen were subjected to a bayonet charge. Those that opted to run were scythed down by their own captured Maxim guns or the Lewis sections occupying gun emplacements. The 13th Brigade war diary states that: 'both assaulting companies had excellent targets as the enemy bolted towards Vimy'.

Now, at around 1400hrs, it was 1st and 2nd Divisions' turn to marvel at the 'green fields beyond' but it was frustrating for the forward artillery observers. Communications links were not yet in place to permit the adjustment of fire onto retreating German artillery limbers and baggage trains.

The first priority was consolidation. Infantrymen cleared the woods on the eastern slopes of the ridge, killing or capturing stragglers. The 27th Battalion managed to grab Major Maier – commander of 3rd Bavarian Reserve Infantry Regiment – with all his staff. German trenches were occupied and improved. Carrying parties from reserve battalions arrived with extra tools, sandbags and small arms ammunition. Platoon-strength outposts were established forward of Brown Line and the first reconnaissance patrols were pushed out into the village of Farbus and beyond to the railway line.

### Consolidation and counter-attack

The atmosphere up on Hill 145 was less triumphant. The 87th had managed to take the German frontline trenches but they were still short of the Black Line and no 4th Division battalion had managed to capture a Red Line position. By about 1400hrs this was becoming clear to Major-General Watson. He took the decision to postpone 10th Brigade's operation to capture 'The Pimple' and warned its commander, Brigadier-General Hilliam, that he might be called upon to attack Hill 145. In 11th Brigade Headquarters, Brigadier-General Odlum was a forlorn figure, distraught at the fate of his battalions. Of 13 runners that he dispatched to collect situation reports, only one had returned.

The confused picture that the runner related was enough to convince Odlum that it was necessary to commit his reserve in a bid to iron out the salient created by the 87th's disaster in the centre. Then at least his exhausted brigade could hand Watson a consolidated Black Line in keeping with what had been achieved by Brigadier-General

Canadian machine-gunners dig their Vickers in to consolidate the ridge. In total, 130 Vickers were tasked with this responsibility. Had the Germans counter-attacked in force, the Vickers would have proved vital. This photograph was most likely taken in the area of 1st or 2nd Division Red Line objective looking north. (IWM, CO 1146)

MacBrian's 12th Brigade to the north. At 1450hrs, Odlum called in the 85th Battalion and issued a warning order, detailing two companies for an assault at 1745hrs. Half an hour later they moved forward to prepare. Watson supported this attack by ordering 47th and 46th Battalions to move into the line and assist with consolidation of gains that had been made to date. Two companies of the 46th were ordered to advance forward of the Black Line to bolster the decimated 78th Battalion on 12th Brigade's front.

Around the same time as Watson and Odlum were attempting to regain the initiative, Byng was considering a strong reconnaissance beyond his successes in the south. At 1440hrs, he contacted First Army Headquarters to apply for the release of a regiment from the 1st Cavalry Division being held in readiness in Arras. Use of cavalry as a contingency had been part of Horne's outline plan but it never appeared in the final operations order from First Army or the Canadian Corps. Consequently, the 1st Cavalry Division was axed from their order of battle on 5 April and given to the Third Army instead. The absence of cavalry from the plan is understandable. It was not consistent with either the notion of Vimy as a limited objective or the heavily timetabled relationship between artillery and infantry. Less clear is why Byng bothered to make this belated application when he must have known that it would never be staffed by GHQ in time.

The idea was shelved and Byng settled on a small reconnaissance of Willerval by the attached squadron of Canadian Light Horse. They were not in a position to exploit beyond Farbus Wood until 1620hrs because, when the order came, they were forcibly settling a dispute by Chinese labourers in the rear areas. Two patrols were formed. One of about 12 horsemen struck towards Willerval. Though it managed to capture ten Germans in the village itself, the appearance of a Maxim gun drove the patrol back to Farbus with the loss of its officer and five troopers. The other patrol fared little better. It moved through Farbus Wood and scouted towards Willerval but ran into an infantry position on the railway embankment and was decimated. Only two men made it back unscathed. It was an inauspicious debut to the battle and the Squadron lost half its remaining horses to long-range sporadic shelling en route back to Mont St Eloi.

Up on Hill 145, the 85th were in position and ready to go. The Nova Scotians were a new unit and to date had only been employed as labourers. This was their chance to prove themselves. Z-Hour was delayed to 1845hrs and then at the last minute, Odlum and the 85th's commanding officer cancelled the barrage because they did not want to harm the wounded in shell holes around the objective. The message did not reach the companies in time. Z-Hour passed and in the absence of shellfire, indecision reigned. After a pregnant pause, one of the companies launched anyway, followed shortly by the other. Struggling through the mud in the gathering gloom, they met with withering fire and the attack faltered. The advance was only maintained by the brave example of the lead platoon commanders. Past the 87th and into the face of the second line, one of those men, Lieutenant Manning, fell wounded and the troops hesitated again. This time, a corporal called Curll discharged the rifle grenade of a wounded comrade and charged towards a machine gun in frenzy, his legs pumping madly in the mire. The defenders saw him coming and fled. He and his section shot

Brigadier-General Victor Odlum (front centre) with his staff officers. In the information vacuum created by the chaos of 11th Brigade's assault on 9 April, Odlum was described as 'distraught' and 'forlorn' about the fate of his men. The frustrations of command without control must have been unbearable but he kept his head, took a calculated risk on the 85th Battalion and stabilized his front. (IWM, CO 2144)

them down. Inspired by this, impetus returned to the attack. As more Germans pulled back, panic spread and the line collapsed. Ninety-two Germans were killed or captured. The remainder fled towards La Folie Wood pursued by whooping Nova Scotians who had to be reined in lest they overextended the advance.

With the 46th hardening up the left flank of Hill 145 and the 85th taking the centre, finally 4th Division was able to consolidate the Black Line properly. Albeit at grave cost, they had carried the day and the crest was theirs.

One would be forgiven for wondering how just two companies could rout an enemy that had proved so stubborn and potent all day in the face of two battalions. The men holding those trenches were from 5th and 6th Companies of 2nd/261st Regiment. German official accounts attest that the forward company – the 5th – was down to just 15 men manning two machine guns when the 87th finally overran the front line. Low on ammunition and exhausted after both three weeks' bombardment and a whole day's fighting, these men had held on while the rest of *Gruppe Vimy* was overwhelmed to their south. Already they had done more than anyone could have expected.

As has been stressed throughout, von Fasbender's men were tenacious soldiers and wherever practicable, local counter-attacks were attempted. At the higher level too, attempts were being made to mount more significant responses. Around 1100hrs, General der Infanterie von Bacmeister put a plan together to recapture Hill 135 using the 262nd Regiment's 1st Battalion (in reserve) and two Sixth Army reserve battalions, 1st/118th Infantry and 3rd/34th Reserve Infantry from 56th and 80th Infantry Divisions respectively. Von Fasbender endorsed the action, ordering General Major von Bechmann's 1st Bavarian Reserve Infantry Division to provide three of its reserve battalions for a second thrust coming at Hill 135 from the south via Farbus.[21] The attack was scheduled for 1500hrs, but the forces were not ready until nightfall and, ultimately, the enterprise never reached fruition because local commanders were not informed of the plan. Major von Rotenhan in command of 262nd Regiment grabbed von Bacmeister's battalions and used them to bolster the *II Stellung* east of La Folie Wood. The Bavarians

The Canadian Light Horse making their way forward. Though their advance was repulsed at considerable cost, German reports of a 'strong cavalry force in Willerval' did much to spread alarm and despondency. (IWM, CO 1149)

3rd Division troops survey the village of Vimy and the Douai plain beyond. The view from the crest of Vimy Ridge was a marvel to men who had stared at its brooding impregnability for so long. Artillery forward observers faced the frustration of being unable to communicate the locations of withdrawing German forces. (IWM, CO 1351)

were commandeered to shore up improvised defences being improved east of the Vimy railway line.

Meanwhile, six battalions were reinforcing *Gruppe Souchez*, including three of its own reserve units from 16th Bavarian Division. Five were kept just to the rear in Bois de Hirondelle and Méricourt while 1st/14th Bavarian was sent to Givenchy. This battalion tried to mount a counter-attack onto the crest of Hill 145 at 2000hrs, but it lacked co-ordination. They did not advance until midnight, became disorientated, and approached the ridge too far north. An alert Vickers gun crew repulsed them easily.

These responses lacked artillery support, communications, and rehearsed contingencies. The Germans were reeling from a defeat they had not expected. Frontline regiments had ceased to exist and senior commanders were paying the penalty for unprepared and dislocated reserves. Kronprinz Rupprecht appreciated this straight away and put a stop to any counter-attacks until further notice. His biggest concern was

Across the Arras front tanks failed to meet the expectations of their exponents. This Mark II has broken down north of the river Scarpe. As seen in the background, cavalry was still the favoured arm for exploitation but where tanks lacked mobility, cavalry lacked protection. (IWM, Q6427)

An 18-pdr. field gun being dragged through the quagmire. This photograph was taken in Flanders but is a superb illustration of the challenge facing the Canadian Field Artillery in their attempts to bring guns forward in support of any exploitation beyond Vimy Ridge. (IWM, Q3007)

the much larger battle raging along the Scarpe River valley and he needed all the troops he could muster.

Allenby's Third Army was making equally unprecedented progress. They too were using the colour-coded objective system, though the lines were deeper in the most part. By the evening of 9 April, all Black, Red and Blue Line objectives had been achieved with the Brown Line reached in some areas. In places, they had advanced as much as 6km. The Germans of *Gruppe Arras* were under considerable pressure. But unlike the Canadians, Allenby was seeking to continue his advance beyond the Brown Line to a Green Line on the 10th. The main challenge in meeting this goal was to move field artillery forward so that they would be in range to support resumption of the offensive. To attempt any advance against prepared defences without it would be folly.

Although an immediate advance was not being considered, Byng also planned to move his guns forward. He needed to protect his gains against counter-attack and also enable subsequent advances should Haig direct him to do so. This was Phase Five of the artillery plan and in many respects, proved the most difficult. When limbered up, a single 18-pdr.

field gun required a team of six horses. Not even tanks had been able to navigate the morass atop Vimy Ridge and the gun teams met the same obstacle. Horses quickly became exhausted and gun carriages sank to the axle. Ammunition carts stood no chance. Phase Five contingencies included plank road construction to create routes over the ridge but they took days to extend. In the short term, there were only two solutions. Trench mortar batteries were 'man portable' and planners had also taken the step of training field gun crews in the use of captured German artillery pieces. When combined with the fire of advanced batteries, these measures would have helped defend the ridge but they were not sufficient to support exploitation.

In the meantime, the infantry on the ridge busied themselves, continuing to consolidate their territorial gains. Communications trenches were improved, proper fire-steps and parapets constructed, enemy dugouts cleared and limited wiring placed forward of positions. Patrolling was extensive in both frequency and reach. Hot rations prepared in the subway kitchens were carried forward and nearly everyone would have managed an hour or two's rest curled up in a groundsheet. The night of the 9th was bleak and cold.

By now, most of the 6,800 Canadians wounded in the assault brigades had been evacuated from the battlefield and were being processed through the medical chain.[22] Again, the subways proved their worth. Forward dressing stations there were well manned and supplied. Wounded could shelter from the elements, be prioritized, stabilized and where necessary sent rearwards to field hospitals by ambulance or light railway. They also dealt with 815 wounded German prisoners.

The Canadians lost 1,660 killed that day, and 979 missing, probably never to be found.[23]

## 10th Brigade tidies the line

By 1800hrs on the 9th, Major-General Watson had issued Brigadier-General Hilliam his warning order to finish the job on Hill 145 with his 44th and 50th Battalions. He could have asked Byng for use of 9th Brigade or the balance of 5th Division but he did not. This might have been on account of pride or an understanding that the consolidation effort was the priority for reserves. At any rate, the confirmatory orders were issued on the morning of 10 April, with a Z-Hour of 1515hrs. Having rehearsed, the two battalions conducted final preparations and moved up to the Black Line through waterlogged and hastily repaired German communications trenches to be in position by 1500hrs. The original barrage plans were repeated on revised timings and opened at 1504hrs with characteristic fury. Assaulting companies climbed out of the jump-off trenches under the cover of an intense final four minutes of bombardment so they were bearing down on the Germans as soon as it lifted. They reached the leading edge of La Folie Wood in just five minutes. The battle for the warrens on those eastern slopes lasted much longer. Chaotic and violent, it was decided by bomb and bayonet, with Lewis guns preventing any German withdrawal to Givenchy or beyond.

On the left, the 50th Battalion were clear by 1545hrs, taking 135 prisoners from both the 261st Regiment and 1st/118th Regiment that had been sent to reinforce them. There were some notable displays of valour in the 50th. The body of Lieutenant Stauffer, a platoon commander, was

found in the midst of over half a dozen enemy corpses. 'A' Company's commander, Major Costigan, was killed administering first aid to a private wounded in the open. Private John Pattison earned a Victoria Cross by silencing a machine-gun nest single-handed. In all, the battalion suffered 229 casualties. Advancing on the right, the 44th took longer, not reporting their objectives as captured until 1700hrs but they did not suffer as badly. With the ridge now fully in Canadian hands, the 47th Battalion relieved the 44th and 50th on the Red Line that night, allowing them to regroup and prepare for the postponed operation to capture 'The Pimple'.

For von Fasbender, the loss of his final foothold on the ridge validated Kronprinz Rupprecht's directive that *Gruppe Vimy* was to withdraw to the *III Stellung* (or Oppy–Mericourt Line) 6km to the east by 13 April. Von Falkenhausen was in favour of using the reserve battalions to make a stand on the *II Stellung* (regimental reserve line) just below the ridge but he was overruled as it was overlooked by Canadian artillery observers on the ridge. As the *Eingreifen* divisions arrived throughout 10 April, they were placed straight into the *III Stellung* as the frontline garrison, supported by their own field artillery. In order to protect the withdrawal, four regiments

**An Advanced Dressing Station in the Third Army area of operations astride the river Scarpe. Casualties arrived here straight from the regimental aid posts in the front line, hence the slightly chaotic atmosphere. The horse-drawn ambulances moved casualties up to the main dressing stations and field hospitals once they had been stabilized. Casualty prioritisation (known as triage) was an ongoing process that started right from the point of wounding. (IWM, Q2010)**

**The Douai plain as seen from the crest of Vimy Ridge on 11th Brigade's axis where the monument stands today. Bois de la Folie is in the foreground; home to the *Hangstellung* dugouts. The Red Line captured by 44th and 50th Battalions on 10 April ran roughly where the road is now. The *III Stellung* is as marked in red. (Author's collection)**

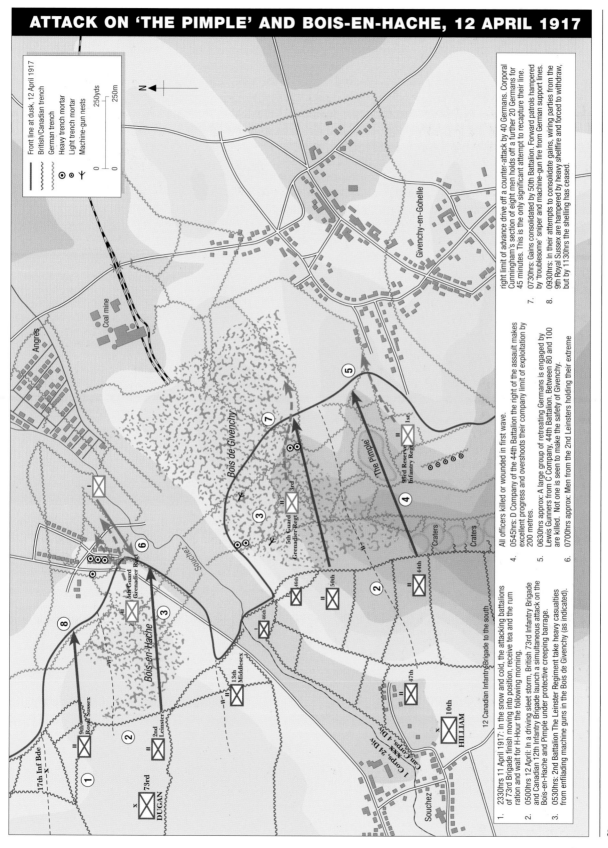

# ATTACK ON 'THE PIMPLE' AND BOIS-EN-HACHE, 12 APRIL 1917

**Legend:**
- Front line at dusk, 12 April 1917
- British/Canadian trench
- German trench
- Heavy trench mortar
- Light trench mortar
- Machine-gun nests

0 — 250yds
0 — 250m

1. 2330hrs 11 April 1917: In the snow and cold, the attacking battalions of 73rd Brigade finish moving into position, receive tea and the rum ration and wait for H-Hour the following morning.

2. 0500hrs 12 April: In a driving sleet storm, British 73rd Infantry Brigade and Canadian 12th Infantry Brigade launch a simultaneous attack on the Bois-en-Hache and Pimple under protective creeping barrage.

3. 0530hrs: 2nd Battalion The Leinster Regiment take heavy casualties from enfilading machine guns in the Bois de Givenchy (as indicated).

4. 0545hrs: D Company of the 44th Battalion the right of the assault makes excellent progress and overshoots their company limit of exploitation by 200 metres.

5. 0630hrs approx: A large group of retreating Germans is engaged by Lewis Gunners from C Company, 44th Battalion. Between 80 and 100 are killed. Not one is seen to make the safety of Givenchy.

6. 0700hrs approx: Men from the 2nd Leinsters holding their extreme right limit of advance drive off a counter-attack by 40 Germans. Corporal Cunningham's section of eight men holds off a further 20 Germans for 45 minutes. This is the only significant attempt to recapture their line.

7. 0730hrs: Gains consolidated by 50th Battalion. Forward patrols hampered by 'troublesome' sniper and machine-gun fire from German support lines.

8. 0930hrs: In their attempts to consolidate gains, wiring parties from the 9th Royal Sussex are hampered by heavy shellfire and forced to withdraw, but by 1130hrs the shelling has ceased.

All officers killed or wounded in first wave.

12 Canadian Infantry Brigade to the south

Angres

Coal mine

Givenchy-en-Gohelle

Bois de Givenchy

The Pimple

98rd Reserve Infantry Regt 1st

5th Guard Grenadier Regt 3rd

5th Guard Grenadier Regt

44th

50th

46th

46th

47th

Craters

Craters

Souchez

Bois-en-Hache

9th Royal Sussex

2nd Leinster

13th Middlesex

10th WILLIAM

73rd DUGAN

17th Inf Bde

I Corps, XXX, 4 Div Can Corps, 24 Div

N

moved forward to reinforce the remnants of 79th Reserve Infantry Division and 1st Bavarian Reserve Division.[24] The 5th Guard Grenadier Regiment (4th Guards Division) went into the line occupied by the 16th Bavarian Division north of Givenchy.

At this stage, von Falkenhausen was keen to hang on to 'The Pimple' (or *Giessle-Höhe* as the Germans called it) as it had utility covering the withdrawal. A much better anchor for their withdrawal was the line at Loos to the north because *Giessle-Höhe* was too far west of Avion. Byng never gave the Germans a chance to debate the issue. An assault on 'The Pimple' was scheduled for 0500hrs on 12 April.

From the outset, General Horne planned a simultaneous attack by 73rd Brigade, 24th Division, north of the Souchez River. In most accounts of Vimy Ridge, this action is ignored. Their objective was the troublesome Bois-en-Hache salient that overlooked British trenches in the river valley and sat across from 'The Pimple'. Commanded by Brigadier-General W. J. Dugan, 73rd Brigade planned to consolidate the German first line as the new brigade front and occupy the captured support trench with outposts. The right flank nearest the river Souchez was to be assaulted by 2nd Battalion, Leinster Regiment, with 9th Battalion, Royal Sussex Regiment, on the northern slopes to the left. The 13th Battalion, Middlesex Regiment, secured the river flank and a battalion of pioneers from the Sherwood Foresters would improve gains and dig communications trenches across the old no man's land.

Up on the high ground to the south of the river Souchez, the Canadian 50th Battalion squared off against the northern portion, reinforced by two companies of the 46th. The 44th Battalion were to the right opposite 'The Pimple' itself and the southern slopes of the spur overlooking Givenchy. They were to maintain a link with the 73rd Battalion on the northern end of Vimy Ridge. Even though they had fought on 10 April, these two battalions were selected because they had rehearsed the attack so many times.

'The Pimple' itself was a dense labyrinth of trenches, bunkers and dugouts, defended by two fresh German units, 3rd/5th Guard Grenadiers on the crest and 1st/93rd Infantry to their south. They had arrived on the evening of 10 April.

Canadian infantry resting in a freshly consolidated trench on Vimy Ridge. Of interest is the selection of personal equipment on display. The nearest Short Magazine .303in. Lee Enfield has the canvas dust cover over the working parts. On the right there is a box of Mills bombs. The figure in the foreground is wearing his greatcoat. This is unusual because men were directed to leave them behind in order to save weight. (IWM, CO 1286)

Both attacking brigades rested on the 11th and moved up to the line from 1930hrs to 2330hrs that night. The Germans suspected an attack and doubled their sentries. It was snowing and bitterly cold. Tea and rum were issued in the early hours and the men assembled at 0400hrs. Z-Hour was not delayed and the barrage opened at 0500hrs precisely. One hundred and twelve 18-pdr. guns worked the Canadian objectives and 46 the British. It was still dark and a strong wind was blowing stinging flurries of snow in the direction of attack. The barrage lifted at Z plus 5 and the assaulting companies went 'over the top'.

As expected, the going was terrible. Mud was waist deep in places. As the men laboured on, Germans emerged from their dugouts. On Bois-en-Hache, both battalions met with a sharp response. Royal Sussex lost five officers and fifty-five men reaching the first line. Not a single officer in the Leinster's first wave made it. Only the cloak of darkness and the foul weather enabled them to reach the first line trenches without crippling losses. The 5th Guard Grenadiers were forced to fight with grenades because it was impossible to acquire targets with a rifle.

To the south, the Canadian 44th and 50th also struggled to maintain momentum in the glutinous conditions. They were moving too slowly at just 20m a minute and lost the protection of the creeping barrage. As with the British, the conditions enabled them to overcome the first line without too much loss but in all cases, the second line proved tougher.

By now, the grey of dawn had penetrated the darkness and German machine guns were able to fire at visual targets rather than on fixed lines.[25] On the slopes of the Bois-en-Hache, enfilade fire from uncaptured Canadian objectives across the river inflicted casualties as well. Neither the Royal Sussex nor the Leinsters consolidated the second line. Instead, they held ad hoc outposts, keeping German counter-attacks at bay while the first line behind them was reconfigured for defence. It was a junior commander's battle. An Irishman called Corporal Cunningham held on to one of the Leinsters' outposts with fanatical stubbornness. Wounded in four places and armed with a Lewis gun and Mills bombs, he single-handedly beat off repeated counter-attacks. When his Lewis gun drum was expended, he threw grenades to suppress the enemy while he changed it. Having accounted for over 20 of the enemy and expended his ammunition, he was compelled to withdraw.

The 44th and 50th reached their second line by 0545hrs, however, as 73rd Brigade attests, it took them longer to silence all the defenders. Damage to second line trenches on the right confused the 44th and they overshot into the Bois de Givenchy, losing touch with the 73rd Battalion to their south. Two young officers – Lieutentants Roberts and Lewis – were sent to make contact but they were never seen again. The war diary also reports that:

> During movement to final objectives on right, a large party, estimated at 80 to 100 of the enemy, ran out of the dugouts in the direction of Givenchy. These men were taken on by the Lewis guns of D Company so effectively that not a single man reached Givenchy.[26]

Retreating Germans being cut down is a scenario repeated often at Vimy Ridge. Nowhere is the sordid ignominy of warfare better illustrated than this episode, recorded so matter-of-factly by the adjutant in the war diary. Like startled game, the flight of that German company would have drawn shouts from the Canadian infantry while Lewis gunners moved into hasty fire positions, adjusting their battle sights. The wet, overcast dawn will have put the scene into flat monochrome and deadened the report of gunfire to a heavy clatter. Laboured breathing and a dreamlike impediment of deep, clinging mud was the German experience, followed by the zip and crack of incoming bullets. All around, men would double up, some silently, others shrieking, as the rounds hit home with a sickening thump. Those that stopped for wounded comrades were easily struck. More agile targets demanded longer bursts, most of the rounds striking wide with angry geysers of mud. Crawling wounded would be left for last, possibly being despatched with single rifle shots. It was grim, ruthless work devoid of the virtues we sometimes associate with combat – courage, sacrifice, determination, and mercy – simply terrified men being put to death by others numbed to the task.

As the morning progressed, the line became quiet and consolidation of gains was possible without molestation from snipers and the occasional shell. The semblance of a counter-attack formed up opposite the 50th at about 1430hrs, but Lewis guns dispersed it. The capture of all First Army's objectives was complete.

**Canadian infantry resting in a frontline trench. The soil is not chalky enough for this to be Vimy Ridge but the photograph is included because it emphasizes the exhaustion of the fighting man. This factor is often underestimated in debates about exploitation of victory. The man in the centre is most likely drawing up a sentry roster. (IWM, CO 2533)**

**8** After 'Vingt Deuxième'
**9** TNA, PRO, WO/95/3838. FLY and FLAPPER are codenames for sections of enemy trench.
**10** TNA, PRO, WO/95/3875.
**11** The only possible exception to this was the Sopwith Pup but only three RFC squadrons were using it in April 1917.
**12** Iron rations were for emergencies and it was an offence to consume them without sanction. They only amounted to hard tack biscuits and tins of bully beef.
**13** Bombers, rifle bombers and Lewis gunners carried 50 rounds.
**14** *Die Osterschlacht bei Arras 1917*, p. 37.
**15** These tactics have hardly changed since then. Though only numbering three sections, the modern infantry platoon is similarly equipped with both belt and magazine-fed suppression weapons, grenade launchers, hand grenades, rifles and bayonets.
**16** *Die Osterschlacht bei Arras 1917*, p. 45.
**17** Some of the mines blown on the Western Front were massive, incorporating up to 50,000lb of ammonal explosive.
**18** *Die Osterschlacht bei Arras 1917*, p. 40.
**19** Canadian Corps slang for Germans.
**20** TNA, PRO, WO/95/1550.
**21** 1st/225 Reserve Infantry, 3rd/6th Bavarian Infantry and 3rd/21st Bavarian Infantry.
**22** The figure excludes men that died of wounds that day and includes the 323 British wounded in 13th Brigade.
**23** A minority might simply have been separated but most were mutilated beyond recognition or buried by shellfire.
**24** 73rd and 164th Regiments (111th Division) went to 79th Division; 89th Grenadier and 75th Regiments (17th Division) to 1st Bavarian Reserve Division.
**25** 'Fixed lines' are pre-registered arcs, enabling guns to fire blind in a set pattern.
**26** TNA, PRO, WO/95/3900.

# AFTERMATH

## CONCLUSION OF THE ARRAS OFFENSIVE

13 April marks the natural conclusion of the battle for Vimy Ridge. Consistent with the schedule imposed by Kronprinz Rupprecht, Sixth Army had executed a general retirement to the *III Stellung* (Oppy–Mericourt Line) the previous night. In the north, *Gruppe Souchez* withdrew east to Avion in a line that ringed the Lens suburbs. Akin to Operation *Alberich* in February, everything of value was destroyed in their wake. This took the Canadians by surprise for corps intelligence staff had interpreted the large number of German reserve forces moving around on the Douai plain as preparations for a counter-attack.

Byng had managed his dispositions accordingly, using 9th Brigade to relieve 7th and 8th Brigades of 3rd Division, and withdrawing 13th Brigade to reconstitute 5th Division as a reserve under unified command. Almost immediately he used them to relieve the beleaguered 4th Division. Vacant German defences were detected by daylight patrols early on the 13th and a tentative advance was ordered in response. Vimy, Givenchy, and Willerval were occupied accordingly. Neighbouring divisions did the same – 51st pushing into Ballieul and 24th into Angres. The fresh German positions were encountered at Arleux and Byng ordered his men to dig in. Horne wanted an immediate assault but clearly this was impractical. Guns were still not forward and the weather was appalling. A pause was necessary.

Haig shared this view and suspended the Arras offensive late on the 14th. Allenby's Third Army had failed to achieve the breakthrough forecast so optimistically. The huge gains of the 9th had not been repeated on the 10th and 11th. VI Corps was successful south of the River Scarpe, reaching their Brown line objectives. Their 37th Division had captured Monchy, 7km beyond the German front line. Further south, the situation was not as positive. VII Corps' 21st Division was beaten back by German counter-attack and nowhere had the cavalry fashioned any significant penetration. For the most part, the infantry were doing what was asked of them, but cavalry were never in place to capitalize. They were not to blame. As ever, communications were problematic and routes were also heavily congested by the effort to move field artillery forward. By the time the cavalry arrived, it was always too late. Both 2nd and 3rd Cavalry Divisions were given tantalizing warning orders only to reach the front and face cancellation or casualties.

Fifth Army's ANZAC attack at Bullecourt was also disappointing. They were facing the new Hindenburg Line manned in their area by the 27th Württemberg Division. Delays were imposed by failure of artillery to breach the wire. Impatient, General Gough was beguiled by the notion that his eight tanks could achieve it alone. The attack was launched prematurely on the 11th. The tanks did not deliver their promise and the Australians were left to proceed unaided even by a creeping barrage. Showing characteristic fortitude and obstinacy, they cut and battled their way into the first line. Having captured it, subsequent attacks against depth positions were gruelling. By the 14th, they had advanced just a costly 2km.

Offensive operations on the Scarpe were resumed on 23 April. These attacks lacked the confidence and preparation of the early effort and were limited in scope, aiming to shape the new front line in the BEF's favour. Gains of up to a mile were achieved in places. The Canadians went into action at Arleux with eventual success (having been driven back from their initial gains). By 24 May, the line settled down. Haig's emphasis had shifted north to his plans for a renewed offensive in Flanders, culminating in the muddy misery of Passchendaele.

## NIVELLE'S FORTUNES ON THE CHEMIN DES DAMES

Early April was fraught with debate about the timing for Nivelle's much-anticipated offensive. The Army Group commander, General Micheler, argued that to launch it at the same time as Haig's would negate the desired effect of drawing away Germany's theatre reserves. This view prevailed and it was agreed that they would attack four days after the British. Various delays were imposed on account of the weather and incomplete artillery fire plans but the attack went ahead on 16 April.

The preliminary attack by *Groupe des Armées du Nord* at St Quentin on 13 April was half-hearted and ended in failure; it nowhere near achieved its aim of sucking in reserves. Unfortunately, the main attack by *Groupe des Armées de Reserve* between Soissons and Reims was to prove equally underwhelming. The root of its failure was a complete lack of surprise – strategic, operational and tactical. Plans had been captured in advance and the preparatory barrages were ponderous, setting a predictable pattern.

As the offensive opened, the initial signs were encouraging. Despite warning, the Germans had front loaded their dispositions again at a loss of 20,000 prisoners. However, this time their *Eingreifen* divisions were well placed. In the main, gains were limited to the forward zone. Though the *Groupe des Armées de Reserve* drove the Germans from the west end of the Aisne valley, seized tracts of the Chemin des Dames and opened the Soissons–Reims railway line, determined German counter-attacks prevented the expected breakthrough.

Therein lies the true cost of French failure at Chemin des Dames. Optimism was so inflated that disappointments were interpreted as disasters. Disillusionment soon followed. Casualties had been heavy – 96,125 by 25 April – but it was the sense of futility that proved so damaging to the survivors. Starting on 29 April, but peaking between 25 May and 10 June, various episodes of 'collective indiscipline' were recorded across 54 divisions. Regiments refused to return to the

Some jubilant infantrymen being ferried back off Vimy Ridge to the rear for a wash, hot meal and one would hope, an almighty blow-out in the *estaminets* of the nearest town. The first troops to be relieved were the 4th Division on 13 April. All troops who took part were given the chance to rest and recover within a week of the battle. (IWM, CO 1405)

Dead French *poilus*. The seemingly futile sacrifices of yet another failed offensive triggered widespread acts of protest in the summer of 1917. (IWM, Q23706)

front; drunkenness and vandalism were prevalent. Aside from specific grievances about treatment of wounded (which had been incompetent) and leave cancellations, the *poilus* were fed up of being assured of quick victory. Ultimately, soldiers respect honesty and competence above all else. Nivelle was relieved and replaced by the charismatic General Pétain, who resurrected morale by addressing many of their demands. Inevitably his response was not bloodless.

# THE CHIMERA OF BREAKTHROUGH

As the 'Spring Offensives' of 1917 closed, Allied commanders could be forgiven for a degree of exasperation. Particularly at Arras, the first day had been so encouraging. Gains had been achieved in a single morning that had taken weeks – and tens of thousands of lives – to achieve the previous year. Breakthrough had been enticingly near but still elusive. Whilst opportunities presented themselves, they were nothing more than a mirage and in this context, Vimy Ridge is at its most illuminating.

A number of accounts carp on about wasted opportunity at Vimy Ridge. On the morning of 9 April, from about 0730hrs to 1130hrs, the Douai plain lay wide open with the Germans in full retreat. It is argued that Byng should have planned for this; the cavalry should have been standing in readiness. Even the infantry could have cancelled the barrage plans and pressed ahead. It is an attractive notion and to debate it is constructive as the episode illustrates the fundamentals of warfare on the Western Front in 1917.

Before any valid examination of these three criticisms, it is worth reaffirming the reasons for the Germans' failure to hold the ridge. The fact that von Falkenhausen kept his *Eingreifen* divisions too far back has been laboured, as has his complacency. In its military manifestation, complacency is a fascinating flaw because often it is brought on by experience. This was especially true of von Falkenhausen, for he had seen the French throw themselves at Vimy and fail, and had witnessed British offensive mining operations come and go without them risking an accompanying offensive. Many of his troops had sat in their dugouts, making themselves at home, since the autumn of 1914. He certainly did not expect to lose – at least not quickly.

Had von Falkenhausen managed to mount a significant counter-attack, it is probable that he would have failed. The First Army had an overwhelming superiority in artillery and the gradient heading west is decidedly unfavourable. Kronprinz Rupprecht recognized this, which is why he ordered the retirement to fresh positions beyond the point that the ridge afforded *decisive* observation. All the same, as far back as they were, the *Eingreifen* divisions were still in a position to react to breakthrough.

Byng's plan was forged in the understanding that Vimy Ridge was to be a limited objective and it is a realistic criticism that he dedicated little effort to exploitation contingencies, preferring to focus on consolidation. No record survives of his thought processes but it is surprising that a pre-war cavalry officer spurned the opportunity to bring 1st Cavalry Division under his command. Arguably, Byng understood the essential limitations of this arm and knew that all advances needed to be patient and deliberate.

A plank road being constructed over broken ground. This is an Australian photograph from Flanders but it is another example of the work that had to be completed before any meaningful advance could be attempted. Against these intrinsic challenges, it is no wonder that 'breakthrough' was so elusive. (IWM, E (Aus) 902)

It is unclear how far Byng's detractors feel the cavalry could have exploited beyond Vimy. They lacked artillery and *matériel* support. They had a voracious appetite for fodder and only rudimentary capability to hold ground. Even if they had somehow breached the *III Stellung*, they would only have come up against the *Wotan Stellung* to its rear and troops reacting with the advantages of interior lines. As demonstrated at Arras and with the Willerval debacle, the timing of their launch also suffered from the inherent shortcomings of battlefield communication.

The notion of infantry exploitation is also unrealistic. It would have meant dispensing with the barrage that so far had been their lifeline but more fundamentally, it would have placed enormous strain on the stamina of the men. They had already achieved a fantastic amount and needed to draw breath.

Byng understood that infantry could only prevail with systematic and well-timetabled artillery support. They needed their cumbersome heavy weapons – mortar and machine gun – to defend their gains. In all respects, they could only advance at the pace of their logistic tail and their artillery. To expect anything more of them would be fanciful. This conclusion was as much a revelation as any of the period's other innovations.

In March 1918, the impasse was broken when the Germans found a winning formula with their stormtroopers but it too proved to be flawed. Once the initial momentum abated, the old rules re-imposed themselves. Eventually, only mechanization, armour and air cover would give commanders the means to exploit success on the modern battlefield. In 1917 (and indeed World War I as a whole) they were still in their infancy. By focussing creativity and setting realistic parameters in the interim, Byng was able to achieve notable success through meticulous preparation and the tenacity of a first class corps.

# THE BATTLEFIELD TODAY

Of all the battlefields that one visits, those of World War I demand the most imagination. The countryside you walk today is the polar opposite of the torn landscape fought over then. Furthermore, the limits on manoeuvre make the study of topography rather bland. Often you have to research battles carefully to extract the significance of a particular knoll, copse or gully.

Along with the forts and hilltops of Verdun, Vimy Ridge is among the most accessible to the mind's eye. Its commanding significance is clear as you crest it and it is also home to an extensive memorial park. In 1922, the French government gave a large portion of the ridge to the people of Canada 'in perpetuity' in recognition of their sacrifice. As such, the ground has been left untouched. Much of it is now forested and off limits on account of the dangers of unexploded ordnance but it is still brought to life in a way that most other Western Front battlefields are not.

The Canadian nation is hugely proud of its victory at Vimy. It was the first time that the Canadian Expeditionary Force had fought together as a corps. In retrospect, that realization of unity was a fundamental expression of nationhood. Consequently, the crest of Hill 145 where the Nova Scotian 85th Battalion relieved the Canadian Grenadiers is now the site of an impressive Dalmation stone monument of which Mother Canada forms a part.

Looking south-west from the monument, they have cut a break through the trees back to the old Canadian front line. This makes it possible to discern the distances involved in 4th Division's assault. Around the monument, the pockmarked ground is still evident, though the shell holes have softened and become shallow with age. Close to the monument there is a visitor centre, which houses a historical display. It incorporates a short film that is informative, even if it is a touch over-patriotic. Outside the visitor centre there is an excellent bronze map in relief, allowing an accurate orientation with the events of 1917.

Approximately 1km south of the visitor centre is the Grange Subway and preserved outpost line of the 3rd Division. It is definitely worth walking between the two because the road makes its way down the old front line past many of the craters from the 1916 mining offensive. Do not ignore the information hut at this end of the park because it contains a small gallery of period photographs and some detritus of the battle in glass cases. The preserved trenches there are an interesting addition. Veterans rebuilt them after the war using sandbags filled with wet concrete. The most important thing to bear in mind as you explore them is that they represent the *outpost* positions around the lips of mine craters in no man's land. The defended front lines were further apart. In this respect the marker boards are misleading. If you look carefully,

The German *Minenwerfer* emplacement in the preserved outpost line of Vimy memorial park. The outposts themselves are forward of this point and the Canadian flag marks the approximate position of the Grange Subway exit. (Author's collection)

you can work out the main positions between 50 and 100m back. Albeit an obvious point, it is also worth considering that in their petrified state, these outposts delineate rather than illustrate. Their greatest benefit is the sensation of being 'below the parapet'.

That said, there are a few points of detail which visitors will find interesting. On the off side of the Canadian trenches are a series of shelves cut into the revetment. These represent the 'funk holes' that soldiers slept in. Only officers, headquarters, and medical posts were afforded the protection of dugouts. The sentry positions are split into two 'fingers'. This was to prevent a single grenade from wiping out both men on duty. You can also see the steel 'sniper plates' that they used for peering down their sights with a degree of protection. On the German side, there is a concrete sentry post and a *Minenwerfer* emplacement.

Most evocative of all is the Grange Subway. It is open from early May to late September and tours are guided by young Canadian volunteers. They are very personable and knowledgeable (even if one did tell me that Byng was a Canadian!). The subway has been improved by replacing timber supports with concrete ones and there is a modern lighting system but otherwise it is much as the tunnellers left it. Claustrophobic visitors should decline the opportunity, especially since thelights are sometimes turned off. When down there, it is not difficult to imagine the men moving around and making their final preparations.

The Grange is the only example restored for access but all the subways and tunnels used by offensive miners are still below the ridge. Many will have collapsed by now – it is impossible to tell – but a specialist volunteer organization called the Durrand Group studies these mining operations and in some instances re-opens galleries. This is in the interest of public safety as well as historical curiosity. Not all the mines were detonated at Vimy Ridge and in 1997, the Durrand Group bored beneath the memorial park to disarm an ammonal charge that had lain dormant since 9 April 1917. Close to the information hut is a modest and touching memorial to Lieutenant-Colonel Mike Watkins, a retired British Army explosives expert who was killed by tunnel collapse attempting to neutralize another mine beneath Vimy Ridge in 1999.

Dedicated enthusiasts may want to see more of the ridge than just the memorial park. In order to do this, it is essential to purchase the 1:25,000 IGN map of north Arras (Series Blue, number 2406E). Marry it carefully with the maps in this book and you can have a fruitful day's exploration. 'The Pimple' is relatively easy to find and a visit definitely improves one's appreciation of its significance. Further south, the village of Thelus is a good landmark. The landscape is more open in that area and possible to find Hill 135, Commandant's House, Bois de Bonval, Goulot and Farbus Wood. The line where the *Zwischenstellung* lay north of Thelus is also discernable in this area.

The village of La Targette boasts a typical French private enterprise war museum, complete with mannequins raided from a discount clothing outlet. Attempt photography at your peril. The lethargic curator will spring into an alarmingly animated state. The area around La Targette was thick with battery positions and a wander will demonstrate the sighting principles discussed earlier.

For a detailed visit, you should buy the World War I battlefield tour guide entitled *Vimy Ridge* by Nigel Cave. Aside from the April 1917

The monument that marks the highpoint of Hill 145. Inscribed upon it are the names of all Canada's dead during World War I. Mother Canada is visible on the left. (Author's collection)

The nationality of this soldier is evident but not relevant. Fascinating as military history is, our anthusiasm must always be exercised with images like this in mind. (IWM, Q 23942).

battle, it points you towards the French memorials on the Lorette Spur and also many of the British operations in 1916. In this instance, you will need to stop over and Arras is the best place to stay. There are plenty of hotels and the main square boasts some tasty little restaurants. In the spirit of so many British soldiers in Arras before me, I over-trained on the brandy and treated the local residents to an off-key rendition of 'Danny Boy' as I meandered back to the hotel. This course of action is not advisable if you plan activity for the next day as the memorial park is best visited first thing in the morning.

Vimy Ridge is only an hour's drive from Calais. Indeed, anyone who has driven along the A26 to Reims will already have seen it because the motorway runs along the western edge at Junction 7. I am also extremely fortunate in having flown over the battlefield in a light aircraft. 16 Squadron's view of Vimy Ridge was a splendid one, though on this occasion, I was grateful for the absence of von Richthofen and his 'Flying Circus'.

However one divides the time spent on Vimy Ridge, it is essential to reflect on one or more of the cemeteries spread across the battlefield. Some mark the old frontline – men having been killed just seconds after clambering over parapets – others are more centralised. There is also a large German cemetery just south of La Targette.

Compelled as we are by military history and the virtues we think that conflict espouses in its combatants, the real language of war is violence, loss and grief. 3,598 Canadians and British were killed on Vimy Ridge between 9 and 14 April. German losses are harder to quantify. An estimate of their fatalities within the same timeframe and area is 2,400. The 3rd Bavarian Division regiments in the line only mustered 200 survivors. Believe it or not, by the standards of that war those losses are 'light', and this is a much-celebrated aspect of the battle. Accurate as that conclusion is, it must never encourage a devaluation of the suffering that the battle inflicted.

# FURTHER READING

## Primary sources

The best primary source material relating to the operation to capture Vimy Ridge is found in the National Archive (Public Records Office) at Kew in London. Their collection of War Office files contains copies of all the operations orders, post-operation reports and war diaries from the First Army down to each battalion. Details of how to access this material are found on their website www.nationalarchives.gov.uk.

Duplicate material for Canadian units is also held in their Public Archive in Ottowa. The website www.archives.ca will point you in the right direction. The battalion war diaries are accessible on-line and you can download the Canadian official history of the Great War from the website www.dnd.ca/dhh. It is an excellent service.

For first-hand eyewitness accounts, the Canadian Public Archive holds a series of detailed interviews tape-recorded for a Canadian Broadcasting Corporation (CBC) programme called *In Flanders Fields*. Private papers and diaries are in abundance and mostly held in Canadian provincial archives.

German primary sources are virtually non-existent. Allied bombing in World War II destroyed the Reichsarchiv in Potsdam. Only limited material relating to Bavarian forces survives by virtue of being held in the Munich archives. The Bavarian Army Museum in Ingolstadt is very forthcoming with assistance. Their website is www.bayerisches-armeemuseum.de.

## Secondary sources

The official histories relating to Vimy Ridge are as follows:

Britain Falls, Captain Cyril, *History of the Great War – Military Operations France and Belgium 1917*, London, 1940

Canada Nicholson, Colonel G. W. L. , *Canadian Expeditionary Force 1914-1919*, Ottowa, 1962

Germany Behrmann, Franz and Brandt, Walter, *Die Osterschlacht bei Arras 1917 – 1. Teil – Zwischen Lens und Scarpe*, Berlin, 1929

The following books offer an informative examination of the battle itself:

Berton, Pierre, *Vimy*, Anchor Canada: Toronto, 1986

Buffetaut, Yves, *The 1917 Spring Offensives*, Histoire et Collections: Paris, 1997

Cave, Nigel, *Vimy Ridge: Arras*, Leo Cooper: London, 1996

Macksey, Kenneth, *The Shadow of Vimy Ridge*, Kimber: Toronto, 1965

McKee, Alexander, *Vimy Ridge*, Stein and Day: London, 1966

Wood, Herbert Fairlie, *Vimy!,* MacDonald and Co.: Toronto, 1967

For a broader perspective on World War I and the individual experience:

Graves, Robert, *Goodbye to All That*, Penguin: Harmondsworth, 2004

Holmes, Richard, *Tommy*, HarperCollins: London, 2004

Jünger, Ernst, *Storm of Steel*, Penguin: Harmondsworth, 2004

Keegan, John, *The First World War*, Alfred A. Knopf: London, 2000

Terraine, John, *The White Heat*, Pen and Sword: Barnsley, 1992

Winter, Denis, *Death's Men*, Penguin: Harmondsworth, 1985

# INDEX

**95**